Books by Quintus Curtius

Translations:
On Moral Ends
On Duties
Sallust: Conspiracy of Catiline and War of Jugurtha
Stoic Paradoxes

Essay Collections:
Thirty-Seven
Pantheon
Pathways

Contributing Author:

The Plutocratic Insurgency Reader

About The Translator

Quintus Curtius is the pen name of writer and translator George Thomas. He graduated from MIT in 1990 and served on active duty for a number of years as a US Marine Corps officer, with deployed service worldwide. After leaving active duty, he enrolled in law school and began to practice law after graduating in 1998. He resides in Kansas City and travels frequently. He can be found at www.qcurtius.com.

LIVES OF THE GREAT COMMANDERS

By

Cornelius Nepos

Translated With Notes And Illustrations

By
QUINTUS CURTIUS

Lives Of The Great Commanders

Copyright © 2019 by Quintus Curtius
All rights reserved.

This book and any portion thereof may not be reproduced without the written permission of the publisher, except for the use of brief quotations for literary reviews.

Cover art by James Seehafer

Printed in Charleston, South Carolina, United States of America

Published by Fortress of the Mind Publications

www.qcurtius.com

ISBN: 978-0-578-58161-3

Whatever withdraws us from the power of our senses, whatever makes the past, the distant, or the future predominate over the present, advances us in the dignity of thinking beings. Far from me, and from my friends, be such frigid philosophy as may conduct us indifferent and unmoved over any ground which has been dignified by wisdom, bravery, or virtue.

—Dr. Samuel Johnson
(From Boswell's *Tour of the Hebrides*)

TABLE OF CONTENTS

Foreword 11
Introduction 16
Lives of the Great Commanders 31
   Preface 32
   I. Miltiades [C. 555 B.C.—489 B.C.] 35
   II. Themistocles [C. 524 B.C.—459 B.C.] 48
   III. Aristides [C. 530 B.C.—C. 468 B.C.] 62
   IV. Pausanias [C. 510 B.C.—C. 465 B.C.] 66
   V. Cimon [C. 510 B.C.—450 B.C.] 75
   VI. Lysander [?—395 B.C.] 80
   VII. Alcibiades [C. 450 B.C.—404 B.C.] 86
   VIII. Thrasybulus [C. 440 B.C.—388 B.C.] 102
   IX. Conon [C. 444 B.C.—C. 394 B.C.] 107
   X. Dion [408 B.C.—354 B.C.] 113
   XI. Iphicrates [C. 418 B.C.—C. 353 B.C.] 123
   XII. Chabrias [?—357 B.C.] 127
   XIII. Timotheus [?—354 B.C.] 131
   XIV. Datames [?—362 B.C.] 136
   XV. Epaminondas [?—362 B.C.] 148
   XVI. Pelopidas [C. 410 B.C.—364 B.C.] 161
   XVII. Agesilaus [C. 445 B.C.—359 B.C.] 166
   XVIII. Eumenes [C. 362 B.C.—316 B.C.] 176
   XIX. Phocion [C. 402 B.C.—C. 318 B.C.] 189
   XX. Timoleon [C. 411 B.C.—337 B.C.] 193
   XXI. On Kings 202
   XXII. Hamilcar [C. 275 B.C.—228 B.C.] 207
   XXIII. Hannibal [C. 247 B.C.—C. 182 B.C.] 212

From the Book on the Latin Historians 227
   XXIV. Cato [234 B.C.—149 B.C.]....................................228
   XXV. Atticus [C. 110 B.C.—32 B.C.] 233
Fragments, Testimonies, and Judgments............................256
Index..262

Foreword

We are told that the philosopher Aristippus was once asked how the educated differ from the uneducated. "Exactly," he replied, "as horses that have been trained differ from those that are untrained."[1] What he meant by this, I think, is that a primary function of education is to shape and discipline one's character. Education in classical times sought to produce well-rounded, productive individuals who would be fit for the responsibilities and challenges of life; character and moral development were held to be just as important as the acquisition of knowledge. Physical and mental training went hand-in-hand, and a student was expected to show progress in both areas. The historian Will Durant found the classical Greek educational program "an excellent combination of physical and mental, moral and aesthetic, training, of supervision in youth with freedom in maturity; and in its heyday it turns out young men as fine as any in history."[2]

The emphasis on character and moral development is a thread running through much of classical and Renaissance writing. The ancient historians, both Greek and Roman, are filled with moral admonitions on the role of Fortune in human affairs, and classical drama unceasingly reminds us of hubris's ruinous consequences. Plutarch saw character as the primary determinant of one's fate, an idea that dates back at least to Heraclitus; his primary concern,

---

[1] Diogenes Laertius II.69.
[2] Durant, Will, *Life of Greece*, New York: Simon & Schuster (1939), p. 290.

he tells his readers, is to explore the personalities of his subjects, not to write history.[3]

This theme of character appears in other fields of discipline as well. Quintilian, that prince of rhetoricians, considered good character a requirement for public speaking, and devotes a special section in his treatise on the subject.[4] "No art, endeavor, or progress," he warns, "will come to anything without diligence, confidence, and personal fortitude."[5] Even the physician Galen was mindful of the importance of character; in his treatise *The Best Doctor Is Also A Philosopher*, he makes it clear that it is vital to the practice of medicine:

> For if in order to discover the nature of the body, the differentiae of diseases and the indications for cures, it is appropriate for him to be practiced in logic, and to stay diligent in the practice of these things, to despise money, and to exercise self-control.[6]

This emphasis on character and moral training was renewed and strengthened during the Renaissance. Paolo Vergerio's 1402 educational treatise *The Character and Studies Befitting a Free-Born Youth* had this to say on the importance of moral instruction:

> The youth should always be kept occupied with some honorable physical or mental activity, for leisure makes young people inclined to lust and every intemperance…But not only is leisure very dangerous to them, but also solitude, which caresses a weak mind with constant thoughts about such things and prevents it from finding diversion elsewhere…They

---

[3] See, e.g., his prologue to the lives of Alexander and Julius Caesar.
[4] *Inst. Orat.* XII.5.
[5] *Id.*
[6] *Quod Optimus Medicus Sit Quoque Philosophus*, I.60K.

should only be entrusted to those whose character and entire life has been thoroughly scrutinized, who do not present an example leading to sin, but possess the authority to deter them from it.[7]

The humanist Franciscus Barbarus, in a 1417 letter to Poggio Bracciolini, states that "When the Athenians consulted Apollo—in their view, the wisest of the gods—they were told that the very best citizens would be those who instructed their children on what was best and most beautiful."[8] Comments like this were not disposable cant. They are evidence of a value system that was taken very seriously, and that illuminated every aspect of educational life.

These educational currents persisted for many centuries. Cornelius Nepos's *Lives of the Great Commanders* occupied a niche not only as a textbook for Latin language study, but also as a tool for moral and character instruction. As some of the illustrations in this book demonstrate, Nepos appeared in countless "school editions" through the 17th, 18th, and 19th centuries. In clear, unadorned language, his short biographical sketches helped readers understand what qualities allowed his subjects to rise to distinction, and what defects eventually caused their downfalls. Moral truths were thereby revealed.

All of this changed in the twentieth century. Dizzying technological transformations, catastrophic world wars, and profound social upheavals all shook the collective faith in traditional educational models. Fashions in literature and art emphasized the

---

[7] Kallendorf, Craig, *Humanist Educational Treatises*, Cambridge: Harvard Univ. Press (2002), p. 21-22.

[8] *Athenienses enim cum Apollinem opinione sua sapientissimum deum consulerent, responsum habuerunt, se praestantissimos cives habituros, si quod optimum, ac pulcherrimum esset, liberorum suorum auribus imponerent.* See *Francisci Barbari et Aliorum ad Ipsum Epistolae*, Brescia: Johannes-Maria Rizzardi, 1743, p. 3.

dynamism and vigor of the Age of the Machine. New priorities came to replace the old, and, with an understandable sense of exhilaration, instructors sought to free themselves from the tyranny of the past. Pedagogy was not immune to these trends: it sought new stimuli, new models, and new sustaining rationales. It is right that such things should happen now and then; periodic revolt refreshes and renews a healthy society's circulatory systems, and prevents the ossification of thought and training.

But as prosperity, money, and the blessings of peace multiplied, the importance of character and moral development began, slowly but steadily, to slip from the collective memory. Nepos, who had once been universally known, became by the late twentieth century universally unknown. Individualism, it appeared, began to take precedence over discipline and the development of sound character. Flushed with the leisure and convenience gifted by modern consumer society, we began to confuse liberty with irresponsible license, and indulged every desire by calling it a right; we concealed personal and institutional debasement behind a protective barrier of money; and a thousand new technological distractions shut our ears to the ancient admonitions against hubris, arrogance, and folly.

There is now a sense that the pendulum has swung too far in one direction, and that we must, to some degree at least, revisit the ancient wisdom. As modern life continues to present us with a myriad of challenges in social organization, leadership, economics, warfare, environmental management, education, and health, the study of character and virtue has never been so necessary. It has been neglected for too long. Wealth, information, and technology are of little use if not guided by disciplined minds imbued with ethical principles.

There has been no accessible, annotated translation of Nepos for many generations, and there has never been an edition that is fully illustrated. This book is intended to fulfill the need for a modern translation of Nepos that can be used both by students and general readers with no prior exposure to the subject matter. It is extensively illustrated, not just with original portrait artwork, but with historical material spanning the 16th to the 19th centuries. Readers exposed to Nepos for the first time will be pleasantly surprised, and will understand why he enjoyed such popularity for so many centuries.

I am grateful to many for their support while this translation was in progress. James Seehafer, who designed the cover art for this book and most of my previous books, was extraordinarily generous with his time. Dr. Michael Fontaine of Cornell University has been a consistent source of support and encouragement for several years, and I have much appreciated his friendship and unrivaled sense of humor. Zeljko Ivic was, as always, a welcome and enthusiastic voice. Caleb Jordan Schulz's original graphite portraits have an elegance that match the dignity of Nepos's prose, and breathe fresh life into the profiles. I was grateful for the generosity of the Classical Numismatic Group, LLC at the final stages of the project.

Finally, I would like to thank the countless readers of my previous translations, whose questions and comments have been much valued in the preparation of this book. We study shoulder to shoulder, and stand together as one.

Quintus Curtius
Overland Park, Kansas
September 2019

Introduction

Cornelius Nepos is one of the more elusive figures of classical Latin literature. He was apparently a native of Cisalpine Gaul; we are not certain of his precise birthdate, or even of his hometown.[9] He may have been born in Pavia (*Ticinum*), but the municipality of Ostiglia (*Hostilia*) has also claimed him as one of its sons. He was a close contemporary of his friend Atticus, who was born in 109 B.C., and he states in his biography of Atticus that he counted himself lucky to have outlived him. A date of 110 B.C. or thereabouts is thus a reasonable guess for the year of Nepos's birth. He probably moved to Rome at an early age to avail himself of the city's advantages in education and cosmopolitan living. He was wise enough to avoid involvement in the bloodthirsty politics of his era, and remained content to observe the drawn daggers from a safe distance. His given personal name (*praenomen*) has not come down to us; he seems never to have used it in his literary work, for the ancient writers who cite him refer to him only as "Cornelius Nepos."

He may have been independently wealthy, for he does not provide explicit details on how he earned his living. Perhaps he was involved in some business dealings with Atticus, who knew everyone and had his fingers in many entrepreneurial pies. We can infer from his writings that he was an urbane, cultured gentleman,

---

[9] Pliny (*Hist. Nat.* III.127) claims he had lived along the banks of the Po. The quote is given at the end of this volume in the section "Fragments, Testimonies, and Judgments."

a type that was well-suited to serious literary activity. He almost certainly knew Greek (as we infer from the preface to his *Lives*), and was able to consult original sources as needed. A comment in one of Cicero's letters[10] to Atticus implies that Nepos suffered the death of a child around 44 B.C. Nepos himself likely died around 25 B.C., shortly after the start of the reign of Augustus Caesar.

He was a prolific writer. We know he composed an epitome of world history in three books titled *Chronica*, which was praised by the poet Catullus. Another of his known works was the *Exempla*, a loose treatise on manners and morals consisting of at least five books; it may have been a work similar to Plutarch's *Moralia*. We know he also wrote biographies of Cato and Cicero, and probably composed some poetry. None of these works have survived; we feel acutely the loss of his *Exempla*, as it certainly embraced a great deal of information about Roman culture and manners. The most extensive and ambitious of his works was a biographical compendium called *De Viris Illustribus* (*On Famous Men*). Nepos can justifiably claim, on the basis of this work, to be the first real biographical writer in Western literature.

The scope of this compilation was impressive. Nepos's plan was to write condensed lives of distinguished men in different fields of endeavor, such as politics, generalship, jurisprudence, rhetoric, philosophy, oratory, history, and poetry. He aimed to include not just Romans, but also famous Greeks, and foreigners of other nationalities. There were at least sixteen titled books in the finished work, each with its own anthology of biographies. The consensus[11] is that it contained the following books:

I. *De Regibus Externarum Gentium* (On the Kings of Foreign Nations)

---

[10] XVI.14.4.
[11] *See, e.g.*, Lindsay, Thomas, *Cornelius Nepos for Sight Reading in Schools and Colleges*, New York: Appleton & Co., 1884, pp. *ix—xii*.

II. *De Regibus Romanorum* (On the Roman Kings)
III. *De Excellentibus Ducibus Externarum Gentium* (On the Great Commanders of Foreign Nations)
IV. *De Excellentibus Ducibus Romanorum* (On the Great Roman Commanders)
V. *De Iuris Consultis Graecis* (On the Greek Jurists)
VI. *De Iuris Consultis Romanis* (On the Roman Jurists)
VII. *De Oratoribus Graecis* (On the Greek Orators)
VIII. *De Oratoribus Romanis* (On the Roman Orators)
IX. *De Poetis Graecis* (On the Greek Poets)
X. *De Poetis Latinis* (On the Latin Poets)
XI. *De Historicis Graecis* (On the Greek Historians)
XII. *De Historicis Latinis* (On the Latin Historians)
XIII. *De Philosophis Graecis* (On the Greek Philosophers)
XIV. *De Philosophis Latinis* (On the Latin Philosophers)
XV. *De Grammaticis Graecis* (On the Greek Grammarians)
XVI. *De Grammaticis Latinis* (On the Latin Grammarians)

The only surviving remnants of this multi-volume pantheon are: (1) the third book, *De Excellentibus Ducibus Externarum Gentium* (literally "On the Great Commanders of Foreign Nations" but more artfully rendered in English as *Lives of the Great Commanders*); and (2) parts of the first and twelfth books. The lives of Cato and Atticus are from the twelfth book, *De Historicis Latinis* (*On the Latin Historians*), and we have a small portion of the first book on foreign kings. The grandeur of Nepos's conception is undeniable, and makes us bitterly regret the mutilated form in which his masterpiece has survived.

These extant portions of Nepos's *magnum opus* have been stitched together by scholars to form the present book, the work we know today as *Lives of the Great Commanders*. In judging what has survived, we must remember that it represents but a fraction of the author's original sweeping vision. His stature as a historian, teacher, and biographer rises significantly once we appreciate this fact.

Lives of the Great Commanders contains the lives of eighteen Greek military leaders, two Carthaginians, a Persian, and a Thracian, along with short summaries of the lives of several foreign kings. The historical period covered by the *Lives* begins about 550 B.C. with the birth of Miltiades, and ends around 182 B.C. with the death of Hannibal. With the addition of the lives of Cato and Atticus, the work in its present form stretches into the Roman republic's final years. Nepos refers to a few of his sources by name, such as Thucydides, Xenophon, Theopompus, Dinon, Timaeus, Polybius, Sosilus, Silenus, and Sulpicius Blitho; some of these names we know, and some we do not. He likely consulted many other authors whose names and works have been obliterated by time. As Nepos makes clear in his sketch of Atticus's life, his book was published several years before Atticus's death in 32 B.C. He published a revised edition a few years later, incorporating additional details into the text.

By the accident of a copyist in late antiquity, Nepos's *Lives* was for centuries mistakenly attributed to one Aemilius Probus, who lived during the reign of the emperor Theodosius I (A.D. 379—395). The first printed edition, appearing in Venice in 1471, perpetuated this error; later editions would follow suit. The Renaissance's spirit of inquiry generated an enthusiasm for critical textual analysis; and in 1569, the scholar Dionysius Lambinus demonstrated that the *Lives* could not have been written during the era of the later Roman empire. Its language, syntax, and overall tone marked it as the product of a much earlier period.

While we may not know many details about Nepos's life, it

turns out that we can infer a great deal about his value system from his writing. We sense he is a man of exemplary character, but without any of the obnoxious severity we find in the elder Cato. We detect no arrogance or vanity in his pages, and he makes no pretension of being a great stylist. He counted Cicero, the poet Catullus (who dedicated a collection of poems to him), and Atticus as his intimate friends. He must have been a man of conspicuous integrity, for no one who was not a solid figure would have lasted long around such luminaries. Nepos may not have been a politician, but he was very close to the best politician of his day (Cicero), and he believed profoundly in both the importance of good character and the injurious consequences of bad character. His summary of Atticus's life paints an unforgettable portrait of the man and his era; so faithful is Nepos to his friend's memory, and so glowing is his depiction, that we feel as if we knew Atticus ourselves. His life of Epaminondas remains one of the key ancient sources of information we have on this brilliant Greek commander, as Plutarch's biography of him has been lost.

There are several recurring themes in Nepos that merit our attention. To understand him, we must understand what was important to him:

1. **Character.** The first of these themes, of course, is human character. "I will demonstrate as best I can," he confidently announces, "that for the most part, every man's character traits determine the trajectory of his life."[12] Of Eumenes he asserts, "If his virtue had received the benefit of good fortune, he would certainly not have been greater than he was, since we evaluate great men by their characters and not by their fortune."[13] Yet Nepos is no brooding fatalist. Character is not fixed at birth; it can be shaped and polished by a determined program of discipline and education, as well as by worldly experience.

---

[12] *Atticus* 19.
[13] *Eumenes* 1.

2. **The Role of Fortune**. While character is critical, it is still subject to the whims of fortune. "For fortune," he warns us, "with her predictable inconstancy, conspired to overwhelm the man whom she had extolled only a short while before."[14] In the sketch on Timotheus he writes: "The variability of fortune is clearly on display in this episode. For the grandson of Conon was forced to restore, from his own funds and with great humiliation to his family, the same walls that his grandfather, using plunder taken from enemies, had reconstructed for his country."[15] Complacency is the undoing of man, and will be punished by fortune's decrees. No one should ever be too assured: "At this point I would like to comment on a principle that is somewhat removed from these events. It is that an overabundance of confidence is often attended by a terrible calamity."[16]

3. **The Fickleness of Human Nature**. Nepos has a guarded suspicion of the masses. He knows that their devotion is subject to recall at any time; and his book is filled with examples of great men betrayed or rejected by those whom they loyally served. Miltiades, for all his labor in the service of Athens, is cruelly shunted aside once his usefulness expired: "In order to appreciate more readily the fact that the nature of all states is the same, we will not stray too far from our subject by relating what compensation Miltiades received for his victory."[17] He then goes on to describe how Miltiades was snubbed by Athens. Datames is led to disaster by an egregious betrayal: "Thus was this remarkable man, who had overcome so many others with superior planning but none with duplicity, ultimately led to ruin by false friendship."[18] Sometimes he is roused to real anger: "In fact, a common defect in great and free republics is that glory's junior partner is jealousy. People love

---

[14] *Dion* 6.
[15] *Timotheus* 4.
[16] *Pelopidas* 3.
[17] *Miltiades* 6.
[18] *Datames* 11.

tearing down those whom they see gaining more prominence over others."[19]

4. **Open-Mindedness**. For a Roman of his era, Nepos is surprisingly open-minded with regard to the customs and mores of foreign peoples. In the Preface to his book he cautions us: "If these readers could grasp that what is morally good and what is objectionable may not be the same for all, and that everything should be judged by the habits inherited from one's ancestors, then they will not be surprised that I have been mindful of the cultural habits of the Greeks in my writings on their virtues."[20] We find this same spirit of openness repeated in the sketch of Epaminondas: "Before I begin my biography of this commander, readers should be cautioned not to form judgments on the customs of other peoples when comparing them to their own ways."[21]

5. **Political Liberty**. There is a strong streak of republican sentiment in Nepos's *Lives*; it percolates just below the surface, and on occasion breaks through in stinging comments. He grieves over the ruin of the Roman republic, and rightly blames ambitious generals, unchecked avarice, and political corruption for its downfall. Consider this passage from his sketch of the life of Agesilaus:

> With this decision, one must admire [Agesilaus's] sense of duty no less than his military virtue; for although he was commanding a successful army and had supreme faith in his ability to defeat the Persian kingdom, he possessed enough self-restraint to follow orders from the absent magistrates—just as if he were a private citizen in Sparta appearing before an assembly. I only wish our own generals could have behaved in similar fashion![22]

---

[19] *Chabrias* 3.
[20] Preface, para. 1.
[21] *Epaminondas* 1.
[22] *Agesilaus* 4.

These sentiments are unsurprising, considering the turbulent age in which Nepos lived. He despises authoritarianism, and has no use for the vain pretentions of aspiring autocrats. In the life of Dion he provides us with a profound truth: "Here, as we have noted before, the bitter resentment that absolute power engenders, and the miserable life of those who would rather be feared than loved, was on display for all to see."[23] In the life of Eumenes, he bluntly states: "Thus there is a great danger that our military men will behave in the same manner as the Macedonians generals, and destroy everything through their lack of restraint and self-serving outlawry—not just those who oppose them, but even the accomplices who aid them in their plans. Anyone who reads about the actions of the Macedonian veterans of that era will detect unmistakable similarities with the events of our own time, and will understand that the only real difference is the intervening gulf of years."[24] In the life of Thrasybulus, he calls attention to his political courage: "Thrasybulus was not only the first man to confront the tyrants openly: he was at first the *only man* to do so."[25]

Nepos clearly read deeply not only in Roman history, but also in the histories of Persia, Greece, and Carthage; his errors when he deals with foreign cultures stem not from animosity, but from undue faith in questionable sources. He is a man of common sense, and finds it difficult to place much confidence in the artifices of honey-tongued rhetoricians and crafty philosophers. He complains in a letter to Cicero:

> I am so far from believing that philosophy can instruct us how to live, and acts as the agent of a happy life, that I think no one needs to learn how to live

---

[23] *Dion* 9.
[24] *Eumenes* 8.
[25] *Thrasybulus* 1.

more than most of these people involved in teaching it. From what I see, a large part of those people in the schools who advocate most cleverly in favor of self-control and abstinence are the same ones living in thrall of all the appetites.[26]

These are the words of a man who has lived through turbulent and dislocating times, and who understands the fearful price exacted by hubris and moral corruption. Nepos is not a "scientific" historian, even by the standards of his day; it is not his purpose to weigh causes, effects, and historical events. He never aspires to be a Thucydides or a Polybius; not only does his biography of Hannibal fail to include an analysis of the battle of Cannae, it barely even mentions the engagement. He sometimes gets dates and places wrong, and probably did not tour Greece or Asia Minor to conduct first-hand researches. On the other hand, he was writing about events that took place hundreds of years before his own time, and likely felt that his investigations were adequate for his objectives, which were moral and ethical, rather than technical and scientific.

And yet, in the final result, none of these shortcomings really matter. We do not read Nepos for analyses of historical causes and effects. What matters to him are *character and moral rectitude*: he seeks to know what made his subjects great, and what flaws led them to decline or ruin. His sketches are not "biographies" in the modern sense, where the writer aims to give a complete summary of a life from birth to death. Nepos is instead giving his readers *his impressions and interpretations* of the lives of his subjects; he wants to highlight the character traits of each man that he believed were decisive.

---

[26] See the section at the end of this book, "Fragments, Testimonies, and Judgments," for the source of this quote.

Like Cicero and Sallust, he came of age during a time of debilitating political corruption and institutional decline; he was disturbed by what he saw around him, and was fired by a desire to educate his countrymen on the importance of character and virtue, so that they might make themselves fit for the stern responsibilities of life and work. Once we understand this, and accept Nepos on his own terms, we can acquire a greater appreciation for what he accomplished.

He remains the first biographer in Western literature, and in some way was a literary visionary. He was the first Roman to write about the lives and deeds of foreign notables. We must remember that he had no predecessor, no prior Roman exemplar, on which he could model himself, and was forced to do the best he could with the tools that were available. The essential goodness of the man is beyond question, and emerges on nearly every page. His biographical sketches, which are neither too long nor too short, somehow persist in the mind long after we have closed his book; and the effect of reading them, one after the other, is to feel the steady, certain pulse of an engine of inspiration.

Antiquity held him in high regard; Suetonius, Pliny, Aulus Gellius, and Ammianus Marcellinus all cited him with confidence.[27] Without doubt he was a significant influence on Plutarch, whose *Parallel Lives* was inspired at least in part by Nepos's work. It is time for our era to acknowledge his achievement, and solicit his insights.

This translation is intended to introduce Nepos to a modern audience that may never have heard of him. It is extensively annotated, as the *Lives* references many historical names and events that benefit from additional amplification. It is also a fully illustrated translation. The illustrations in this book are of two types: (1) Caleb Jordan Schulz's portraits, commissioned especially for

---

[27] See the final section of this book, "Fragments, Testimonies, and Judgments" for a selection of these quotes.

this volume, of Dion, Epaminondas, Hamilcar Barca, Hannibal, Lysander, Pausanias, Themistocles, Timoleon, Alcibiades, and Aristides; and (2) various historical illustrations from the 16th to the 19th centuries that add to the reader's perspective and enjoyment by showing the timelessness of Nepos's material.[28]

In the table of contents and with each biographical sketch, I have included in brackets each figure's dates of birth and death. Obviously, these are not part of Nepos's text. But since they can assist readers in placing each name in historical context, I have included them here.

A number of editions of the Latin text of Nepos were consulted in the preparation of this translation: Ortmann, Eduard, *Cornelii Nepotis Qui Exstat Liber De Excellentibus Ducibus Externarum Gentium*, Leipzig: Teubner (1891); *Cornelii Nepotis Quae Extant Omnia*, Turin: Joseph Pomba (1835); Fischer, J., *Cornelii Nepotis Vitae Excellentium Imperatorum*, London: A.J. Valpy (1822); Chambers, R., *Cornelii Nepotis Liber De Excellentibus Ducibus Externarum Gentium, Cum Vitis Catonis Et Attici*, Edinburgh: Wm. & Robt. Chambers (1852).

---

[28] These historical works are: Sebastian Münster, *Cosmographia* (1546); Christopher Wordsworth, *Greece: Pictorial, Descriptive, and Historical* (1839); August Meissner, *Leben des Epaminondas* (1814); and Guillaume Rouillé, *Promptuarium Iconum Insigniorum* (1553).

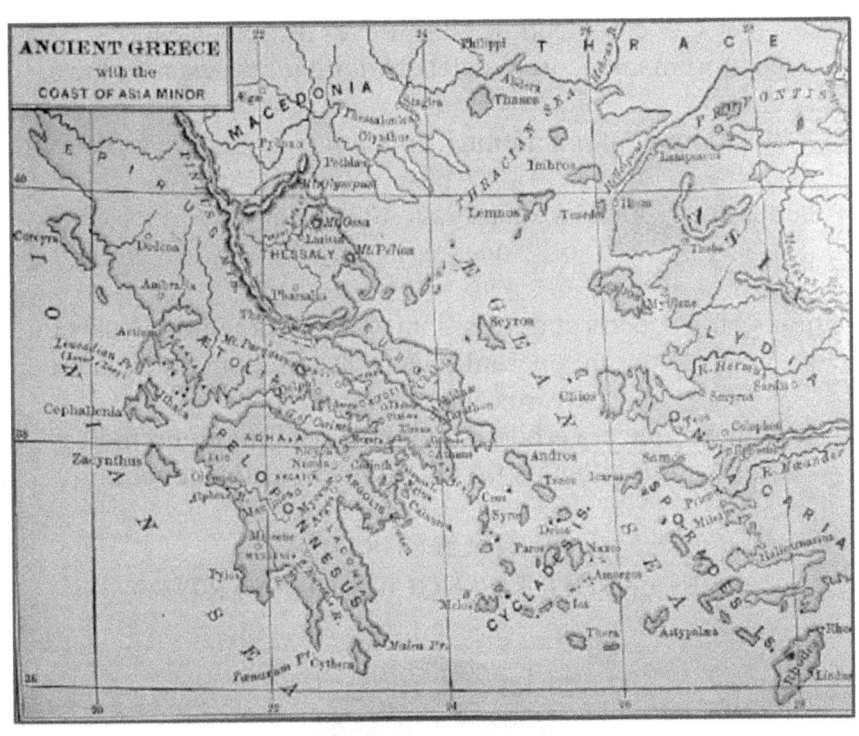

Map of ancient Greece, showing locations mentioned in Nepos's text

CORNELII NEPOTIS
LIBER
DE EXCELLENTIBUS DUCIBUS
EXTERNARUM GENTIUM

Ad usum scholae accommodatus.

Qui complectitur vitas breves describentes
imperatorum Graecorum celeberrimorum res gestas et facta.

Qui illustratur cum praefatione, animadversionibus, adnotationi-
bus
doctissimis, propriis adumbrationibus, atque iconibus supra
quadraginta.

Utilitas huius operis et dispositionis ratio in praefatione habetur.
Fragmenta suorum operum selecta, et testimonia iudiciaque
ex variis auctoribus addita.
Rerum quoque et verborum maxime memorabilium indices
accesserunt locupletissimi, ut inspicienti patebunt.

QUINTUS CURTIUS
RECENSUIT ET ANGLICE CONVERTIT.

CAROLOPOLI:

ANNO MMXIX

Excudebat *Castellum Mentis* Typographus.

LATINARUM LITTERARUM
HORTATORIBUS ATQUE ADIUTORIBUS EXIMIIS
HANC QUALEMCUMQUE LUCUBRATIONEM SUAM

D.D.D.
QUINTUS CURTIUS
AUCTOR

Ad rem iudicandam animis mentibusque nostris ducimur.

LIVES OF THE GREAT COMMANDERS

PREFACE

Atticus, once my readers learn who taught Epaminondas music, or see it noted among his virtues that he was an accomplished dancer and an expert flutist, I have no doubt that most of them will judge this type of writing to be unimportant, and beneath the dignity of great men's characters. But these opinions will generally come from those lacking proficiency in the Greek language—the types of people who believe that nothing is acceptable unless it agrees with their own personal lifestyles. If these readers could grasp that what is morally good and what is objectionable may not be the same for all, and that everything should be judged by the habits inherited from one's ancestors, then they will not be surprised that I have been mindful of the cultural habits of the Greeks in my writings on their virtues.

It was not considered morally reprehensible for Cimon, the great man of Athens, to wed his own sister, since his people accepted this practice; but for us such an act would be judged an abomination.[29] In Crete it is considered laudable for a youth to

---

[29] A misleading statement that requires explanation. Nepos may be referring to old Greek laws that removed certain degrees of consanguinity as a legal bar to marriage. Philo of Alexandria (c. 20 B.C.—50 A.D.) mentions such laws in his treatise *De Specialibus Legibus III* (*On the Special Laws III*): "Therefore the Athenian lawgiver, Solon, when he permitted men to marry their sisters by the same father, forbade them to marry those by the same mother. But the lawgiver [Lycurgus] of the Lacedaemonians, on the other hand, allowed of marriages between brothers and sisters by the same mothers, but forbade those between brothers and sisters by the same father." (*Id.* at IV.22; *see*

experience as many romantic relationships as he can. At Sparta there is no unmarried woman—no matter how well-bred—who cannot be brought to a formal dinner as a paid entertainer. Practically everywhere in Greece, being called the victor at Olympia was viewed as something worthy of the highest praise: even taking the stage and presenting oneself to the public was never seen by these people as a discreditable act. For us, however, all such conduct is considered either deplorable, or seamy and darkened with the tint of scandal.

Yonge, C.D., *The Works of Philo*, Peabody: Hendrickson Publishers (2016), p. 596). However, the existence of these laws does not mean such practices were "accepted." As the *Dictionary of Greek and Roman Antiquities* observes, "Thus brothers were permitted to marry with sisters…if not born from the same mother…though a connection of this sort appears to have been looked on with abhorrence. In the earlier periods of [Greek] society, indeed, we can easily conceive that a spirit of caste or family pride, and other causes such as the difficulties in the way of social intercourse, would tend to make marriages frequent amongst near relations and connections. (Compare [the Biblical Book of] *Numbers*, xxxvi). At Athens, however, in the case of a father dying intestate, and without male children, his heiress had no choice in marriage; she was compelled by law to marry her nearest kinsman not in the ascending line; and if the heiress were poor the nearest unmarried kinsman either married her or portioned her suitably to her rank." *See* Smith, Willian (ed.), *Dict. of Gr. & Rom. Ant.*, London: John Murray (1875), p. 736. The old marriage codes dated from a time of high male mortality rates due to warfare, pestilence, and accident. Presumably they sought to provide a means of subsistence for widows who had few options for remarriage outside their families; they may also have arisen as a means of preserving inheritance and property rights. In practice such marriages must have been extremely rare. Plutarch (himself a Greek) reports (*Cimon* 4) that Cimon was alleged to have married his half-sister Elpinice, and the biographer treats the matter as shameful. The allegation may have been political slander, but the fact that it was viewed by Plutarch as scandalous demonstrates that such unions were anything but accepted. We also note that Plutarch considered reprehensible Ptolemy Philadelphus's supposed marriage to his sister Arsinoe (*On Education* 14).

Conversely, many things that are socially acceptable according to our customs are seen by the Greeks as offensive. Indeed, what Roman would be ashamed to bring his wife to a dinner gathering? What lady of the house does not confidently occupy her home's atrium, and mix with general society?[30] But they do things much differently in Greece: for no woman there is invited to a dinner party unless it is a gathering of extended family. Neither will she show herself outside a specific interior part of the residence called the "woman's chamber,"[31] to which no man may gain admittance unless he is part of her immediate relations. However, the magnitude of the literary task before me, and my eagerness to begin discussing the relevant material of this work, prohibit me from further digression. We will press ahead with our subject, and in the pages that follow relate the lives of the great commanders.

---

[30] I.e., greet visitors who visit the house during the day.
[31] The word used is *gynaeconitis*, a Latinized Greek term.

I. Miltiades [C. 555 B.C.—489 B.C.]

1. Due to the antiquity of his lineage, the renown of his ancestors, and his own self-effacing personality, Miltiades the Athenian (son of Cimon) became one of the most illustrious men of his time. He had reached an age in which not only were great expectations placed on him, but also his fellow-citizens could trust that he actually possessed the strength of character that they believed him to have, when a situation arose in which the Athenians wanted to send colonists to the Chersonesus.[32] Since there was a large number of potential colonists, and many wished to take part in the settlement project, a hand-picked group of them was sent to Delphi to consult with Apollo[33] and determine who would be their most suitable leader.

At that time, however, the Thracians held these regions, and the intended expedition would certainly provoke conflict with them. The Pythia[34] specifically told the delegates that they should appoint Miltiades commander; if they did this, she said, their undertaking would succeed. Having received this answer, Miltiades sailed for Chersonesus with a hand-picked group of men. When

---

[32] Meaning that when he was a youth, people had high hopes for him, and when he grew into manhood, the hopes became firm confidence. Miltiades supposedly traced his lineage to Codrus, the last king of Athens. But the commander who led the expedition to Chersonesus was not Miltiades the son of Cimon, but an uncle of the same name, Miltiades the son of Cypselus. Chersonesus is the ancient name of the Dardanelles peninsula in modern Turkey.
[33] I.e., the Delphic Oracle in Phocis.
[34] The priestess who issued the oracles at Delphi was given the name Pythia.

he had reached the island of Lemnos, he wished to bring the inhabitants under Athenian control, and proposed that the Lemnians submit voluntarily to this arrangement. Ridiculing him, the islanders responded that they would do this when Miltiades set sail from his home and arrived at Lemnos by the wind of Aquilo.[35] But that wind, originating in the north, directly opposes those traveling to Lemnos from Athens. Not having the luxury of wasting time, Miltiades continued with his mission and arrived at Chersonesus.

2. After a short time there he routed the forces of the barbarians. Once he carved out the area he desired, he secured different places with fortifications, settled the colonists he had brought with him, and satisfied their needs with repeated sallies to plunder his neighbors. In these activities he was helped not so much by good judgment, but by luck. For when he had crushed the enemy forces by making good use of his soldiers' fighting prowess, he set up his community according to the highest standards of justice, and resolved to stay there on a permanent basis. His people accorded him the honors of a king, although that title was never used; and his position was never based more on power than on his sense of justice. Neither was he any less outstanding in his duties to Athens, the place from where he had come. Because of this favorable situation, he consolidated a lasting authority with the endorsement of those who had sent him that was no less strong than the approval of those who had gone with him to Chersonesus.

Once he had arranged his affairs at Chersonesus, he returned to Lemnos and, citing the pact he had previously made with them, demanded they deliver the city to him.[36] For they had said they

---

[35] Aquilo was the Roman name for the Greek god of the north wind, Boreas. Lemnos is to the north of Miltiades's home, Athens. Going from Athens to Lemnos would thus not be possible using the north wind, since it blows southward.

[36] Lemnos had two towns, Hephaestia and Myrian. Nepos does not say which town is meant.

would surrender themselves when he left his home and came to Lemnos using the north wind: and now, of course, his residence was located in Chersonesus.[37] The Carians,[38] who then inhabited Lemnos, were paralyzed by these developments. Defeated not so much by their earlier promise but by the good fortune of their adversaries, they dared not resist Miltiades, and abandoned the island. He brought the other islands of the Cyclades[39] under Athenian control with comparable ease.

3. During this same time the Persian king Darius[40] resolved to wage war on the Scythians, and conveyed an army from Asia to Europe. He constructed a bridge across the Hister[41] river over which he led his forces; once he had left, he posted high-ranking commanders he had brought with him from Ionia and Aeolis[42] to guard the structure. He had given each of these men permanent power over cities in their respective regions. He thought this would most effectively allow him to retain control over the Greek-speaking inhabitants of Asia: for if he assigned the protection of Greek towns to his friends, there would be no chance of their personal safety if he, Darius, were ever removed from power.

Miltiades himself numbered among these men. When various informants told him that Darius's campaign was going badly and

---

[37] And due to this fact, he had now sailed north to south, and had used the north wind.

[38] The Carians were a western Anatolian people living along the Ionian coast. *See* Herodotus I.171.

[39] The Cyclades are a group of islands in the Aegean Sea. Their name is derived from the fact that they formed a "circle" around the island of Delos, which was venerated as the sacred birthplace of the gods Apollo and Artemis. However, Lemnos is not considered part of the Cyclades.

[40] Darius I (c. 550 B.C.—486 B.C.), also known as Darius the Great. His invasion of Scythia was in response to their attacks on Persian territory.

[41] The Danube. Hister (or Ister) was its ancient Greek name.

[42] Aeolis was located in the west and northwest coast of Asia Minor (i.e., the southern part of Mysia).

that he was encountering stiff resistance from the Scythians, Miltiades encouraged the guardians of the bridge not to let slip away an opportunity for liberating Greece that had been given to them by fortune. For if Darius and the forces he had brought with him were destroyed, not only would Europe be safe, but the ethnically Greek inhabitants of Asia Minor would also be freed from Persian domination and danger. This could easily be made to occur; for once the bridge was destroyed, Darius would be neutralized in a few days either by enemy action or by the stoppage of supplies.

A stylized 1546 image of siege warfare, from Sebastian Münster's Cosmographia

While many endorsed this plan, Histiaeus of Miletus argued against its implementation. He stated that the position of those holding senior commands was not comparable to the position of the masses; for they relied on the royal authority of Darius to sustain their commands. For once Darius's power vanished, their own authority would evaporate, and they would then face retribution from their own people. He was so adamantly opposed to the plan offered by the others that he believed nothing was more expedient than the continuation of Persian rule. When this view came to be endorsed by the majority, Miltiades left Chersonesus and returned to Athens—certain that since so many individuals had been involved in the discussions, his proposed scheme[43] would soon find its way to Darius's ears. Although Miltiades's plan came to nothing, it ought very much to be commended, for he proved himself more devoted to the well-being of his people than he was to the preservation of his personal position.

4. Meanwhile, Darius returned to Asia from Europe and was egged on by his associates to bring Greece under his control. He assembled a fleet of five hundred ships and assigned its command to Datis and Artaphernes; he also provided them with two hundred thousand infantry and ten thousand cavalry. The purported reason for his aggression against the Athenians was that the Ionians—with Athenian aid—had attacked his garrison at Sardis, killing the men there.[44]

The king's commanders came ashore at Euboea[45] and seized Eretria without delay; they then rounded up all the local citizens and sent them to Darius in Asia. After this they advanced on Attica, leading their forces into the plain of Marathon, a spot that is

---

[43] I.e., the scheme about destroying the bridge.
[44] Sardis was a city in Lydia; its modern Turkish name is Sart. The attack on the garrison occurred in 499 B.C.
[45] This was in 490 B.C.

roughly ten miles from Athens.⁴⁶ The Athenians, inflamed by this sudden crisis which was at once so great and so imminent, sought assistance only from the Lacedaemonians, and sent to Sparta a man named Phidippus (a messenger from that special group of runners known as "express couriers"⁴⁷) to announce how urgently help was needed. At home they selected ten commanders, among them Miltiades, to take charge of the army. There was significant disagreement among them, however: some wanted to take up defensive positions within the city walls, while others wanted to seek out the enemy for a conclusive engagement. Miltiades alone forcefully advocated that they should take the military initiative as soon as possible. If this were done, he believed, the morale of the citizenry would be raised when they sensed that their fighting spirit had not sagged; and the enemy would be more likely to hesitate for the same reason, once they became aware that the Greeks dared to fight them with such a small army.

5. No city offered the Athenians any help at this time except the Plataeans,⁴⁸ who sent a thousand men. With their arrival the number of soldiers swelled to ten thousand; and it was a force burning with a barely-concealed lust for combat. The result of this situation was that Miltiades's plan of action became more persuasive than the plans of his colleagues. Urged to action by his authority, the Athenians brought their forces out from the city and pitched camp in a suitable location. On the following day, the Greek forces organized themselves in battle formation at the foot of the mountain in an area that was lightly obstructed (in fact there

---

[46] The actual words are *milia passuum decem*, literally "ten thousand paces." The Roman mile was equal to 1000 paces, or 4850 English feet. *See* Allen & Greenough's *New Latin Grammar*, Newburyport: Focus Publishing, 2000, p. 425.

[47] The word is *hemerodromos*, an import from Greek which means "day runners." I have opted to translate it as "express courier" to distinguish it from the regular word for courier appearing in this sentence, *cursor*.

[48] A town in Boeotia.

were scattered trees in various places). They then readied themselves to engage the enemy. The operative plan was that, while being protected by the size of the mountains, they would impede the enemy's advance by making use of the trees, in order to avoid being surrounded by the Persians' greater numbers.[49]

Although Datis saw that the terrain was not advantageous for his forces, he was nevertheless hungry for battle and confident in his army's numeric superiority—and even more so since he judged it expedient to fight before the Spartans arrived to render aid. Thus he led his hundred thousand infantry and ten thousand cavalry in battle formation and commenced fighting. The Athenians so surpassed their adversary in military virtue that they shattered an army ten times larger than their own, and terrified them to such an extent that the Persians ran not to their camp, but back to their ships. No more impressive battle in history has yet been fought; and never has so small band of fighters struck down such a powerful adversary.

6. In order to appreciate more readily the fact that the nature of all states is the same, we will not stray too far from our subject by relating what compensation Miltiades received for his victory. Just as honors for the Roman people in olden days were infrequent and modest and therefore highly prestigious, and in our own era extravagant and meaningless, so we find this situation to have been the same for the Athenians long ago. Miltiades, who had secured the liberty of all of Greece, was rewarded only with this honor: when a representation of the Battle of Marathon was painted in the portico known as the Poicile,[50] his image was given first place among the ten military commanders depicted, where he was shown exhorting his men to action and committing them to battle.

---

[49] By having the mountains pressed at their backs, the Greeks hoped to prevent the Persians from surrounding them.

[50] This Latin name is derived from the Greek word for multi-colored. A famous colonnade in Athens, it was the same place where Zeno, the founder of Stoic philosophy, would give lectures.

Yet this same people, after it had acquired greater power and been morally corrupted by the financial doles of the Athenian magistrates, authorized three hundred statues for Demetrius of Phalerum.[51]

7. After this battle the Athenians again gave Miltiades command of a fleet of seventy warships so that he could wage war on the islands that had assisted the barbarians. During his tenure as commander, he saw to it that many islands[52] were brought back under Athenian control; with a few of them, this task had to be accomplished by force. The island of Paros[53] was one of these: emboldened by the extent of its resources, it could not be subdued with dialogue. So Miltiades led his men from their ships, surrounded the city with siege-works, and entirely blockaded it; then, after arranging mantlets and *testudines*,[54] he moved against the city walls. When he was just about to capture the town, a grove of trees far off on the mainland,[55] but still visible from Paros, began to burn one night. The cause of the fire was not clear, but when the flames were seen by the Parian townspeople and the Athenian attackers, both sides assumed it was some kind of signal given by the king's naval infantry.[56]

---

[51] The statesman who ruled Athens from 317 B.C. to 307 B.C.
[52] Meaning islands in the Cyclades.
[53] Located in the Cyclades.
[54] A mantlet is a moveable screen used by soldiers advancing on fixed positions. A *testudo* ("tortoise," with plural form *testudines*) is an armored formation achieved when infantry group together and interlock their shields to deflect projectiles.
[55] I.e., the Asiatic mainland.
[56] The word used is *classiarii*, which can be translated as marines, sailors, or naval infantry. Miltiades feared he was about to be attacked by the Persians.

Frontispiece from a 1675 edition of Nepos

The result of this was that the Parians were deterred from any thought of surrender. Miltiades, fearing that the king's fleet was headed towards the island, burned the siege works he had made and—to the supreme displeasure of his countrymen—sailed back to Athens with all the ships he had brought with him. Thus he was charged with treason. The Athenians believed he could have captured Paros, but had been corrupted[57] by the king and had withdrawn in an abandonment of his mission. At this time he was suffering from the effects of wounds received during the assault on the town; and because he was unable to speak on his own behalf, his brother Stesagoras spoke for him. The verdict of the trial was that he should not be sentenced to death, but instead should pay a fine assessed in the amount of five hundred talents—the same amount of money had been spent in raising his fleet of ships. Because he did not have the resources to pay this fine at the conclusion of his case, he was cast into the public prison and died there.

8. Although he was blamed for the Paros debacle, there was in fact another motive guiding the campaign against him. Because of the tyranny of Pisistratus,[58] which had held sway only a few years before, the Athenians were wary of too much power aggregating in the hands of any of its citizens. It did not seem to them that Miltiades, having held so many military positions of such power, would be able to return to private life—especially since the long experience of command had habituated him to exercising authority.

During all those years when he was living in the Chersonesus, he had become accustomed to unquestioned authority; he had been called a tyrant, but he was a just tyrant. His power was not derived from force, but flowed from the goodwill of his people; and he maintained his standing through benevolence. All men are

---

[57] Through bribery.
[58] Pisistratus held power in Athens roughly from 560 B.C. to 527 B.C.

considered tyrants (and have this name attached to them) who maintain permanent rule in a city-state which once enjoyed the benefits of liberty. But Miltiades possessed such a high degree of compassion, and such a remarkable sense of kinship with his fellow-citizens, that there was no one so lowly who could not gain permission to see him.

He was a prestigious figure in all the Greek city-states; his name commanded respect, and he had earned the greatest possible glory on the field of battle. Yet when his people reflected on his capabilities and potential, they preferred that he should be punished—despite posing no present danger—rather than that they should be burdened by fear of him.

An 1839 image of the Hymettos mountain range in Attica.

II. Themistocles [C. 524 B.C.—459 B.C.]

1. Themistocles, the son of Neocles, the Athenian. The vices that attended his formative years were replaced by such virtues that no one ever surpassed him, and few are considered to be his equal. But our account of his life must start from his origins. His father Neocles was of noble birth. He took as a wife an Acarnanian[59] girl who was a citizen, and Themistocles was the offspring of this union. His conduct as a youth was met with strong disapproval by his parents, for he pursued a libertine lifestyle and paid no attention to his finances. The result was that his father disinherited him. Instead of breaking him, this humiliation only fortified his determination to succeed. Since he believed that this indignity could be expunged only with the most intense effort, he completely devoted himself to politics, cultivating friends and notoriety with focused diligence.

He participated in cases before the law courts,[60] and often appeared in the people's assembly; no important civil matter could be accomplished without him. He could quickly perceive what was needed in a situation, and was able to communicate his thoughts effectively to others. He was no less efficient in executing his plans than he was in formulating them: to paraphrase Thucydides, he judged present conditions with great shrewdness and drew inferences about the future with a remarkable acuity. By

---

[59] Acarnania was a coastal region of west-central Greece lying southwest of Aetolia.
[60] *Iudicia privata*, meaning legal matters generally.

using this skill, he achieved renown within a short period of time.[61]

2. The war in Corcyra[62] gave him the first opportunity for a position of real responsibility. Selected by the people to supervise the conduct of the war, he promptly raised their level of military readiness not only for the present conflict, but also for the future. At that time the public funds derived annually from Athenian mining interests were being wasted by the lavish spending of the magistrates; but he convinced the people instead to use this money to construct a fleet of a hundred warships. This was efficiently done. He first crushed the Corcyreans, then secured the maritime routes by routing the pirates who infested the seas. The result was that he not only enriched the Athenians, but made them skilled in the techniques of naval combat. With the advent of the war against the Persians, the importance of this Athenian naval prowess would become clear to all of Greece.

The Persian king Xerxes[63] had decided to wage naval and land war against all of Europe with forces larger than any other commanded by one man before or since. He had a fleet of one thousand two hundred warships, accompanied by two thousand tenders;[64] his army was reckoned at seven hundred thousand infantry and four hundred thousand cavalry. When reports of the invasion made their way to Greece, and rumors circulated that Xerxes was specifically targeting Athens because of the Persian defeat at Marathon, the Athenians consulted the oracle at Delphi to learn what the right course of action should be.

The Pythia told the emissaries that they should protect themselves with wooden walls. Since no one could decipher the

---

[61] Nepos's source for these comments is Thucydides I.138.
[62] Themistocles's first major campaign was against Aegina (modern Enghia), an island in the Saronic Gulf.
[63] Xerxes I (519 B.C.—465 B.C.) was the son of Darius, and was king from 485 to 465 B.C.
[64] Meaning transports or "vessels of burden" (*naves onerariae*).

meaning of this response, Themistocles convinced his people that Apollo's instructions were that they should secure themselves and their moveable property within ships—for this was the significance of the deity's phrase "wooden wall." Once this decision was made, they added an equal number of triremes to the number of vessels previously noted, and conveyed everything that could be moved either to Troezene or Salamis.[65] They left Athens's Acropolis[66] to the priests and a few elderly people, who were tasked with performing the traditional religious ceremonies. The rest of the city was abandoned.

3. This plan dissatisfied many of the other city states, who preferred to join battle with the enemy on land. For this reason an elite force was sent under Leonidas, king of the Lacedaemonians, to occupy Thermopylae[67] and block any further barbarian advance. They were unable to contend with the strength of the invaders, and all of them were killed in that place. But the unified Greek fleet of three hundred vessels—of which two hundred were Athenian—first clashed with the Persian king's naval infantry at Artemisium, which is located between Euboea and the Greek shoreline. Themistocles was seeking a narrow strait so that he would not be enveloped by the enemy's greater numbers. Although both sides ceased fighting without a clear victor, the Greeks nevertheless dared not remain in this place: for there was a danger

---

[65] Salamis (now called Coluri) is an island in the Saronic Gulf off the coast of Greece. Troezene is now a Greek town named Damala in the Argolid Peninsula.

[66] Nepos uses the single word *arx* (citadel), but to insert this bland term would insult the fame of the Acropolis.

[67] The narrow coastal pass at Thermopylae ("place of hot springs") is one of the few land routes into southern Greece. The battle that took place there is, of course, one of the most famous in history. Leonidas held the pass for two days until he was betrayed by a local man who showed the Persians a path that could be used to outflank the Greek force. To prevent a full envelopment, Leonidas sent away most of his force, and remained in place with 300 Spartans to guard their retreat.

that if part of the enemy fleet sailed around Euboea, they would be facing an attack from two directions. For this reason they withdrew from Artemisium and positioned their fleet at Salamis, which faces Athens across the water.[68]

4. Meanwhile Xerxes, having fought his way through Thermopylae, immediately advanced on Athens by stratagem; and since it had no defenders, he slaughtered the priests who had taken refuge in the Acropolis and burned the city. The fires in Athens aroused such fear among the soldiers at sea that they dared not stay where they were; most of them strongly wished to withdraw to their homes and take up defensive positions within their own walls. Themistocles alone disagreed with this course of action. He insisted that if they remained united they could stand against the enemy, but swore that if they divided themselves, they would all die: and he made it clear to Eurybiades,[69] the Lacedaemonian king who then held the highest military authority, that this was the stark reality of the situation.

But Themistocles was less persuasive with the Spartan than he had expected. He therefore sent one of his most trusted servants at night to make contact with the Persian king; the servant's task was to convey a message from Themistocles that the Persian's adversaries were about to flee. If they scattered their forces, the war could only be finished with greater effort and time, since the Persian king would be forced to subdue each city state separately; but if Xerxes attacked them immediately, he would swiftly crush them all. Themistocles's intention here was to force all the hesitant Greek city states to fight the invaders. Having heard this message, the barbarian king did not believe any ruse was being employed against him. Although the king's military position was quite disadvantageous—and the position of the Greek defenders very

---

[68] I.e., Salamis is an island in the Saronic Gulf located a short distance (16 km.) to the west of Athens. Nepos here uses the rare word *exadversum*, meaning "vis-à-vis" or "over-against."
[69] He was not the king, but the Spartan naval commander.

favorable—he nevertheless engaged the Greek fleet on the following day in waters so narrow that he was unable to deploy his ships effectively. For this reason Xerxes was defeated; and this outcome was more a product of Themistocles's wise counsel than it was a result of Greek military prowess.

5. Although things had gone badly for the Persian king, he still possessed such reserves of manpower that he might be able to crush his enemies. Yet he was thwarted a second time by the same man. Themistocles, dreading that Xerxes would want to continue fighting, made sure word was conveyed to the king that the bridge he had built at the Hellespont was about to be destroyed, an event that would prevent him from getting back to Asia. Xerxes was persuaded of the truth of this rumor. So while his original passage into Greece had taken place over a six-month period, he withdrew into Asia over the same line of march in less than thirty days: and he was assured that Themistocles had not outmaneuvered him, but had in fact done him a valuable service. Thus through the prudence of one man was Greece made free, and thus did Asia concede defeat to Europe. This is a second victory which can be placed alongside Marathon as a trophy. For at Salamis, just as happened before,[70] the greatest naval force in historical memory was defeated by a small number of ships.

6. As magnificent as Themistocles was in that war, he proved to be no less great in peace. The Athenians were using the harbor at Phalerum, which was both unsuitable and too small; on his recommendation, the triple port of Piraeus[71] was built and ringed with such solid defensive works that it rivaled Athens in excellence, and surpassed her in usefulness. He also restored Athens's city walls, an undertaking that involved considerable risk to himself. For the Lacedaemonians—having been handed a suitable

---

[70] "Just as happened before" (*pari modo*) refers to the Battle of Marathon, but the comparison is only valid in the sense that a large Persian force was defeated by a small number of Greeks. Marathon was not a naval engagement.

[71] Piraeus is north of Phalerum. It was a "triple port" in the sense that it contained three separate depressions.

pretext (i.e., the barbarian invasions of Greece) for insisting that no city outside the Peloponnesus should have defensive walls so that there would be no fortified strongholds a future invader could occupy—made a concerted effort to prevent the Athenians from building city walls. Their professed reason for advocating this policy was, of course, quite different from their true reason. The Athenians, by virtue of their two major victories at Marathon and Salamis, had gained such renown among the Greek-speaking peoples that the Spartans realized it would be the Athenians with whom they would now have to fight for primacy. They therefore wanted the Athenians to have as few defenses as possible.

Once they heard that the walls were under construction, they sent envoys to Athens in an effort to stop the project. With the Spartan envoys in the city, the Athenians halted work on the wall, and said that they would send their own emissaries to Sparta to discuss the issue further. Themistocles agreed to perform this mission and initially departed alone; he urged the remaining envoys not to leave Athens until its walls had risen high enough to protect the city adequately. Meanwhile everyone, including both freemen and slaves, should exert themselves to the fullest, sparing no place—whether religious, public, or private—from scrutiny, and should scrounge from all sources whatever materials were suitable for the construction. It was for this reason that the walls of Athens consisted of material taken from shrines and tombs.

7. However, when Themistocles came to Lacedaemon he declined to seek an audience with the magistrates; he took pains to delay that event as long as possible, citing as a reason that he was waiting for his colleagues to arrive. The Lacedaemonians complained that construction work on the wall was continuing, and that he was attempting to mislead them about this fact. The remainder of Themistocles's envoys arrived in the meantime. When he heard from them that not much work on the walls was still left to be done, he made an appearance before the Spartan ephors, the

body that held the ultimate power.⁷² He informed them that they had been provided false information and, due to this fact, the proper course of action was to send to Athens reliable men of high rank, men whom they knew were trustworthy, to conduct an inquiry into the matter. In the meantime, he said, they could detain him as collateral. Themistocles's proposal was accepted, and three envoys engaged in the most important leadership positions were dispatched to Athens. He ordered his colleagues to accompany them, instructing that the Lacedaemonian legates were not to leave Athens until he himself had been released from custody.

Once he believed that this group had arrived at Athens, he addressed the magistrates and senate⁷³ of the Lacedaemonians and openly informed them that the Athenians, pursuant to his instructions and their own initiatives grounded in the common law of nations, had surrounded with walls the Greek deities, the Athenian state shrines, and the household gods, in order to be able to defend them more easily.⁷⁴ This action by Athens, he maintained, was in no way disadvantageous to Greece as a whole. He told them that his city was a bulwark standing against the barbarian tide, against which two of the Persian king's fleets had already been shipwrecked. He stated that the Lacedaemonians were behaving wickedly and unjustly: they cared more about doing what preserved their own dominance than pursuing policies that were advantageous for all the Greek peoples. So if they hoped to see again the ambassadors they had sent to Athens, they ought to release him; otherwise their envoys would never set foot back in Sparta again.

---

[72] The ephors were five magistrates elected annually. They shared power with the two Spartan kings.

[73] The Spartan senate (*gerusia*) was composed of thirty senators who held lifetime office.

[74] I.e., they were protecting the gods worshipped by all of Greece, the gods specifically venerated at Athens, and the gods of each citizen's household (*penates*).

A sixteenth century portrait of Themistocles

8. Yet he did not escape the ill-will of his own people. The focus of the same fear that had damned Miltiades, he was expelled from the city as a result of votes cast by potsherds, and left to take up residence in Argos.[75] Because of his many achievements, he lived there as a man of considerable standing; but the Lacedaemonians sent envoys to Athens who charged him—without giving him an opportunity to respond—of having made an alliance with the king of Persia to gain control of Greece. He was condemned for treason *in absentia* as a result of this accusation.[76]

Once Themistocles was made aware of this, he realized that he was no longer safe in Argos, and relocated to Corcyra. When he saw that the ruling faction there was afraid his presence would give the Athenians and Spartans an excuse for declaring war, he went to see Admetus, king of the Molossians,[77] with whom he had a cordial host-guest relationship.[78] When Themistocles arrived there, the king happened to be absent; and in order to impose a greater duty on Admetus of taking him in and providing sanctuary, he took hold of the king's young daughter and took refuge in a shrine that was cultivated with the utmost reverence. He did not remove himself from that place until the king had given him his right hand and guaranteed his safety.

The king honored his word. For when the Athenians and Lacedaemonians publicly demanded that he hand over the sanctuary-seeker to them, he did not comply. He warned Themistocles to consider his situation: it would be not be easy for him to live in

---

[75] This voting by potsherds or shells was a peculiar Greek custom. A citizen considered too potentially powerful could be banished from Attica by fellow citizens voting on pieces of broken pots or shells. Six thousand votes in favor were enough to condemn a man to exile.

[76] This happened around 466 B.C.

[77] A Greek people located in Epirus.

[78] *Cum quo ei hospitium erat. Hospitium* indicates a "permanent relationship between host and guest," and the "ties of hospitality," according to the Oxford Latin Dictionary. It was considered a very important bond, with an implied offer of sanctuary adhering to it.

safety in a place so close to Greece. Admetus therefore ordered him to be escorted to Pydna, and provided him with an adequate personal security guard. There he boarded a vessel in which the entire crew was ignorant of his identity. When a violent storm carried the ship to the island of Naxos[79]—where the Athenian army was then stationed—Themistocles realized that if he came ashore there he would certainly perish. Compelled by necessity, he disclosed his identity to the ship's captain, and promised to reward him generously if he would save him. Aroused with sympathy for the plight of such an illustrious man, the captain anchored the ship at sea far from the island for a day and a night, and would not permit anyone to leave the vessel. From there he sailed to Ephesus and deposited the fugitive safely ashore. Themistocles later rewarded the captain for his actions.

9. I know many writers have asserted that Themistocles crossed into Asia during the time Xerxes was on the throne. But I give more credence to the opinion of Thucydides, for he was closest to Themistocles's age in comparison with other historians of those times; they also both came from the same city. Thucydides writes that Themistocles went to Artaxerxes and delivered a letter to him that contained the following language: "I, Themistocles, have come to you, the man who of all the Greeks brought the most misfortunes upon your house, as long as I was required to fight your father and defend my country. But after I found myself in a secure position and he had fallen into danger, I also did many good things for him. When he wanted to return to Asia after the Battle of Salamis had been fought, I was careful to inform him by letter that the bridge he had built across the Hellespont would be destroyed, and that he himself would be surrounded by enemies. He had been saved from peril by my message. But I am now hunted by all of Greece; I am appealing to you for protection, and seek your friendship. And if I should get it, you will have in me

---

[79] Located in the Cyclades.

no less steadfast a friend than your father found in me an implacable enemy. But as for these issues I want to discuss with you, I request that you give me a year's time and permit me to approach you once that period has elapsed."

10. The king, respecting his greatness of spirit and very much wanting to acquire such a man, granted Themistocles's request. He focused all his time on acquiring the Persian language and literature; and he achieved such a high level of proficiency in these that he is said to have spoken the language more correctly before the king than did those who had been born in Persia. Although he made the king many promises, the one most pleasing to Artaxerxes was that if he, the king, would listen to Themistocles's advice, he would be able to launch a successful military conquest of Greece. After having been given a great deal of compensation from Artaxerxes, he returned to Asia and domiciled himself at Magnesia.[80] The king had presented this city to him with the words, "It will provide you your daily bread," since five hundred talents in revenue came from this region every year; the king also gave him Lampsacus,[81] where he could take his wine, as well as Myus,[82] where he could draw his provisions.[83]

Two monuments erected in his memory have been preserved to the present day: the sepulcher near the town in which he was laid to rest, and a statue that stands in the forum at Magnesia. A great deal has been written by various historians on the way in which he met his death, but here again we should place our faith in what Thucydides tells us on the subject. He says that Themistocles's death came about as a result of an illness at Magnesia. But he did not deny there were rumors that Themistocles had ingested

---

[80] A city in Ionia, near the river Maeander (modern Tekin in Turkey).
[81] An ancient Greek city on the Asian side of the Hellespont (modern Lapseki in Turkey).
[82] A Greek city in Caria along the Ionian coast (modern Avşar in Turkey).
[83] *Ex qua obsonium haberet.* According to the Oxford Latin Dictionary, *obsonium* can mean a "pension allowance" as well as provisions or victuals.

poison, because he had no hope of fulfilling the promise he had made to the king about conquering Greece. Thucydides also claims that his bones were interred in Attica by his friends in secret, since his previous conviction of treason there legally prohibited a public burial.

A clash of armies, from Münster's Cosmographia *(1546)*

An 1839 depiction of mountain travel in Greece

III. Aristides [C. 530 B.C.—C. 468 B.C.]

1. Aristides the Athenian, the son of Lysimachus, was approximately the same age as Themistocles. He was thus destined to contend with him for political leadership. There was in fact much acrimony between them. From their interactions one may truly learn the extent to which eloquence can prevail over moral rectitude. Although Aristides so excelled in moderation that he is the only man in historical memory (at least as far as we are aware) who was given the name "The Just," he was nevertheless brought to ruin by Themistocles, and condemned to a ten year sentence of exile by that notorious potsherd voting custom mentioned earlier.

Indeed, when Aristides learned that the aroused rabble could not be restrained, he noticed, as he was accepting his fate, someone writing on a potsherd that he should be forced to leave the country. He is said to have asked the man why he voted as he did, or rather what act Aristides had committed to merit such a punishment. The man responded by saying that, although he did not know Aristides, it bothered him that Aristides had so exerted himself to be called "The Just" in preference to other men.[84]

He did not serve out the legally-mandated expulsion period of ten years. When Xerxes marched into Greece,[85] he had already

---

[84] Plutarch tells a slightly different version of this story (*Aristides* 7). In this version, an illiterate citizen asked Aristides to write his name on the potsherd. Aristides asked the man what harm Aristides had ever done him. The man said, "None, but I am just tired of hearing him called 'The Just' everywhere." Aristides said nothing, wrote his name on the shard, and gave it back to the man. The reader may reflect on what this anecdote says about the jealous nature of man, and on ingratitude in general.

[85] In 480 B.C.

been expelled for about six years; he was then permitted to return home through the enaction of a public ordinance.

2. He was present at the naval battle at Salamis, which took place before he had been released from his punitive exile. Aristides was also the Athenian commander at Plataea[86] in the battle[87] where Mardonius[88] was routed and the barbarian army was annihilated. There is no other deed of comparable fame in his military record besides the account of that command, but there are many examples of his justice, fairness, and integrity. For it was when he was serving aboard the combined Greek fleet with Pausanias[89] (the leader who had crushed Mardonius) that clear naval supremacy shifted from the Lacedaemonians to the Athenians. Until that time the Lacedaemonians were the dominant naval and land power. But the effect of Pausanias's tactless, autocratic behavior, and of Aristides's sense of justice, was that nearly all the Greek city-states decided to ally themselves with Athens and select them as their leaders in the struggle against the foreign invaders.

3. In order to thwart the barbarians more easily (if by chance they tried to make war on Greece again), Aristides was tasked with finding out what funds each city-state should give for the construction of a fleet and the raising of an army. This task he accomplished; and by virtue of his good judgment, funds totaling four hundred sixty talents were conveyed every year to Delos.[90] The city-states desired this location as their common treasury; all of the money, however, was brought to Athens at a later date. There is no more reliable evidence of his sense of restraint than the fact that, although he had been in charge of such important matters, he died in such a condition of penury that he left hardly

---

[86] Near the modern town of Plataies in southeastern Boeotia.
[87] In 479 B.C.
[88] The Persian military commander who died at the Battle of Plataea.
[89] In 477 B.C.
[90] Delos is an island in the Cyclades in the Aegean Sea. The temple of Apollo there was used as financial depository, a practice not uncommon in antiquity.

any funds to provide for his own burial. The consequence of this was that his daughters were maintained by public assistance; the state treasury took care of them by making adequate provision for their dowries.[91] He died about four years after Themistocles had been expelled from Athens.[92]

---

[91] *De communi aerario dotibus datis collocarentur.* Meaning that the state did not want the daughters of so great a man to be reduced to poverty, and so agreed to supply dowries. There was a specific building on the Acropolis in Athens, called the Prytaneum, that took care of supporting those who had provided exceptional service.
[92] In 468 B.C.

Aristides

IV. Pausanias [C. 510 B.C.—C. 465 B.C.]

1. Pausanias the Lacedaemonian was a great man, but displayed divergent traits in all facets of his life;[93] for although he was distinguished by virtue, he was still riddled with vices. His most well-known achievement was his performance at the Battle of Plataea.[94] For it was under his leadership that Mardonius (a son-in-law of the Persian king, a satrap,[95] and an ethnic Mede,[96] who was among the very best Persians when it came to military prowess and shrewd advice), along with his hand-picked force of two hundred thousand infantry and twenty thousand cavalry, was defeated by a Greek force of greatly inferior size. The enemy commander himself was slain in that battle.

Having won wide acclaim as a result of this victory, he began to embroil himself in many unrelated ambitions, and to covet a good deal more. Among the most important of such incidents was when he was reprimanded for setting up a golden tripod—taken as military plunder—at Delphi. It was inscribed with an epigram that conveyed the following idea: that the barbarians had been routed at Plataea as a result of his generalship, and that he had

---

[93] *Sed varius in omni genere vitae fuit.*
[94] In 479 B.C. a Greek force, led by Pausanias, defeated Xerxes's general Mardonius at Plataea.
[95] An administrative unit of the Persian empire.
[96] He was a Persian, not a Mede, and he was the son-in-law of Darius, not Xerxes.

given this offering to Apollo as a result of his victory.⁹⁷ The Lacedaemonians removed these verses, and inscribed nothing else except the names of the cities with whose help the Persians had been beaten.

2. After this battle the Spartans again sent Pausanias with a joint fleet to Cyprus and the Hellespont in order to drive out detachments of barbarians from these areas.⁹⁸ Having experienced the same good luck in this enterprise, he began to act even more haughtily, and to strive towards ever greater goals. For once the city of Byzantium was taken, he captured a number of Persian nobles and a good many of the king's relatives; these family members he privately returned to Xerxes, feigning that they had escaped from official custody. With them went Gongylus the Eretrian,⁹⁹ who was supposed to deliver to the king a letter inscribed—according to the history of Thucydides—with the following words: "Pausanias, the Spartan commander, when he learned that some of the prisoners captured at Byzantium were members of your extended family, sent them to you as a gift, and wishes to be formally linked to your house through marriage. To this end, if you are inclined to it, please provide him a daughter as a bride. If you do this, he promises that Sparta and all of Greece will, with your help, be reduced to your control. If these suggestions are of interest to you, make arrangements to send him a reliable envoy with whom he may speak."

The king rejoiced at news of the safety of so many family members. He immediately sent Artabazus¹⁰⁰ to Pausanias with a letter praising him and requesting that he carry through what he had promised the king; if Pausanias were to do this, then nothing

---

⁹⁷ Meaning that Pausanias had a verse engraved on the tripod that gave him all the credit for the victory. This was seen as arrogant and offensive, and so the words were removed.
⁹⁸ This was in 477 B.C.
⁹⁹ Eretria was a town on the island of Euboea.
¹⁰⁰ He was a Persian who had escaped from the Battle of Plataea.

he asked for would be denied. Once Pausanias understood the king's designs, he dedicated himself with greater intensity to his own plans—and this aroused the mistrust of the Lacedaemonians. The end result was that he was called back home, formally charged, and acquitted of any capital offense; nevertheless, he was punished with a substantial fine, and for this reason was not permitted to return to duty in the fleet.

3. Not long after this, however, he returned to the army on his own volition, and disclosed his intentions in a way that was more irrational than well-considered. He renounced not only the habits of his ancestors, but also his native garb and culture. He adopted the manner of a king, and clothed himself as a Mede; a Persian and Egyptian entourage obsequiously followed him around. He took his meals according to Persian custom, and in a way more luxurious than his companions could endure. He would not agree to meet with those who came to see him; he responded arrogantly in conversation; and he exercised his power cruelly. He had no desire to return to Sparta, but moved to Colonae, which is located in the Troad; and there he devised schemes poisonous not only to his country, but to himself.

Once the Lacedaemonians became aware of these developments, they sent envoys to him with a ciphered message[101] on which it was written, in their method, that if Pausanias did not return to Sparta, he would be sentenced to death. Unsettled by this communication, and hoping he could ward off peril with money and political influence, he returned home. As soon as he arrived, the ephors promptly had him placed in irons. According to their laws, any ephor may take such action against a king. He secured his own release, but a cloud of suspicion still hung over him: a

---

[101] The word used is *clava*. It was a wooden rod on which was wound a strip of leather or fabric. A message was written on the material, which became unintelligible when unwound. It could only be read by a recipient with a winding-rod of the same dimensions. The cipher is primitive, but effective enough.

belief still lingered that he had a secret partnership with the Persian king.

There is a certain category of men called helots, whose number is extensive; they work the fields of the Lacedaemonians and carry out the tasks of slaves. He[102] was believed to be inciting them with hopes of liberation. But because there was no clear evidence upon which an accusation could be based, his countrymen did not believe that such an important and well-respected man should be tried on suspicions alone; they thought they should wait until events made themselves clear.

---

[102] Pausanias.

A Romantic 1839 depiction of the Greek countryside

4. There was, meanwhile, a certain youth of Argilus with whom Pausanias had had an amorous dalliance when he was a boy. He received a letter from Pausanias for Artabazus, and suspected that something about himself was written in it, since no one previously sent on such deliveries had ever come back. He loosened the wrapping of the letter, broke its seal, and learned that he would certainly perish should he deliver it. There were allusions in the letter related to an understanding that had taken place between Pausanias and the Persian king. The youth turned the letter over to the Spartan ephors.

One must be mindful of the Lacedaemonians' sense of restraint in this situation. Not even this evidence persuaded them to take Pausanias into custody; and they did not believe he should be subjected to coercion until he exposed his own culpability. Thus they instructed this confidential informant what they wanted done. At Taenarum[103] there is a shrine to Neptune which the Greeks believe is profane to disrespect; the informer fled there and seated himself on the temple's altar. Close to this place they excavated an underground cavity from which could be heard anyone speaking with the Argilian youth. Some of the ephors went down into this listening post.

When Pausanias learned that the Argilian had fled to this altar, he himself went there in a greatly agitated state. When he saw the youth seated at the altar as if he were a suppliant, he asked him the reason for such an unexpected consultation; the Argilian then disclosed what he had learned from the letter. Becoming even more alarmed, Pausanias started to beg him not to incriminate someone who was worthy of the utmost consideration; and if he would grant him this favor and support him in his current crisis, he would give the youth a substantial reward.

5. Once the ephors learned of these events, they thought it would be better to take him into custody in the city.[104] Having appeased the Argilian, or so he believed, Pausanias and the youth

---

[103] Now called Matapan, and located in Laconia in southern Greece.
[104] I.e., in Sparta.

left the temple and were returning to Lacedaemon. Right before he was to be arrested along the way back, he realized they were about to spring a trap on him—he gathered this from the facial expression of one of the ephors who was trying to warn him. Running only a few paces ahead of the men chasing him, Pausanias sought refuge in the temple of Minerva[105] (which goes by the name Chalcioicos). To prevent his leaving the building, the ephors immediately barricaded the temple's folding doors. They then demolished the roof, so that he might die more quickly when exposed to the open air.

We are told that Pausanias's mother was alive at this time. When she learned of her son's crimes, she was—despite her age—among the first to bring a stone to the temple's gate to wall in her son. When carried out of the temple he was only half alive; and he took his last gasp of air soon after this. And so did Pausanias disgrace his supreme glory in battle with a contemptible death. After his end, there were some who said that his remains should be brought to the place designated for those who had received formal punishment; but most disapproved of this idea, and they buried him some distance from the place where he had died. In response to a Delphic oracle at a later date, his remains were exhumed and reburied at the actual place where he had expired.

---

[105] Athena.

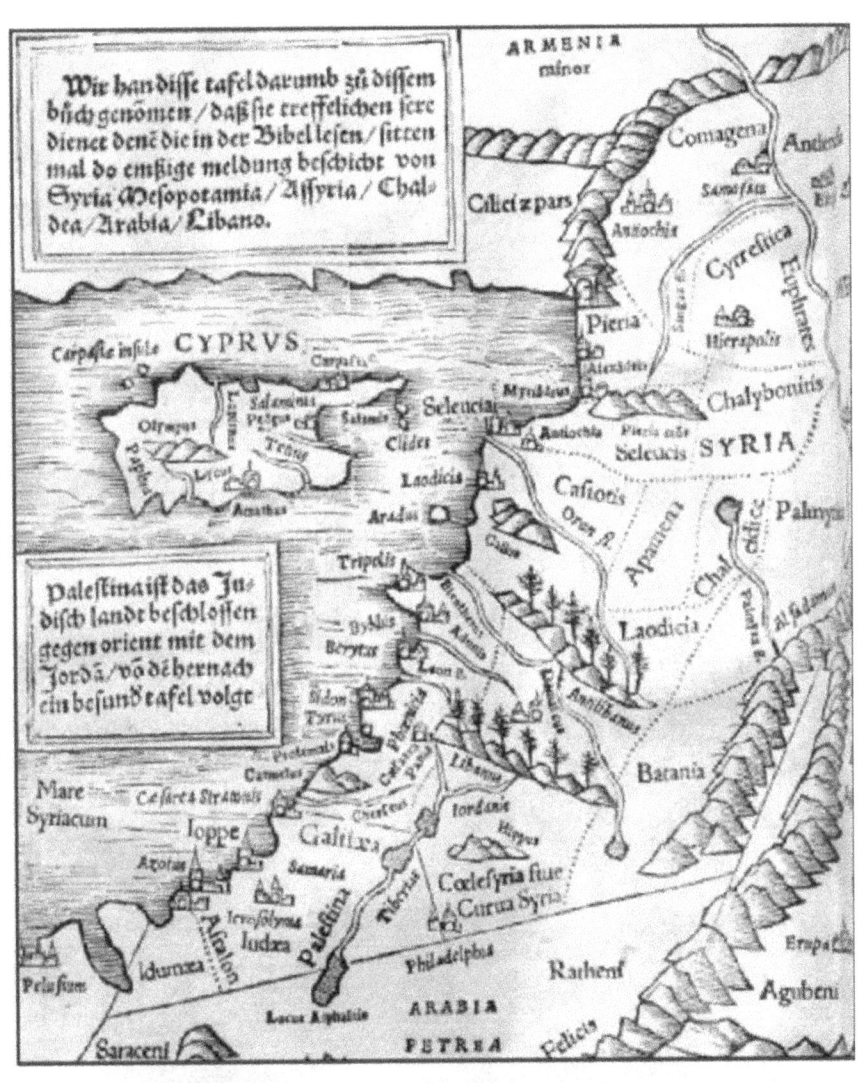

A 1546 map of the Eastern Mediterranean, from Münster's Cosmographia

Pausanias

V. Cimon [C. 510 B.C.—450 B.C.]

1. Cimon the Athenian, the son of Miltiades, had a very difficult start as a youth. His father had been unable to satisfy the fine levied against him by the people, and for this reason he had been hauled off to prison. Cimon was also held in custody, for according to the laws of Athens he could not be released unless he satisfied the fine that his father had been ordered to pay. Guided not more by love than by custom,[106] he took in marriage his own sister Elpinice; for according to Athenian custom, one is permitted to marry sisters born of the same father.[107] A man named Callias, who had wealth but did not come from a distinguished family, wanted to marry her; he had made a considerable sum of money from mining. He begged Cimon to give her to him as his wife, telling him that if he granted this request, he would liquidate Cimon's fine. Although Cimon rejected this idea, Elpinice refused to allow the son of Miltiades to die in prison when it was within her ability to prevent it; so she made it clear that she would wed Callias if he followed through on his promise.

2. After securing his release in this way, Cimon quickly achieved the highest position of state leadership. He was gifted with eloquence, a pronounced generosity, and a good deal of learning in civil law and military affairs; for since his youth he had traveled with his father on his army assignments. He thus held

---

[106] Nepos's words have a poetic feel: *non magis amore quam more ductus*.
[107] As stated in the notes to Nepos's introduction, this statement is misleading. It is likely a political slander that time has turned into legend.

sway over his city's population, and exerted considerable authority within the army.

In his first experience as commander, he put to flight a substantial Thracian force at the river Strymon,[108] and established the town of Amphipolis; he then sent ten thousand Athenians to colonize the area.[109] In his next engagement, he took possession of a squadron of two hundred Cypriot and Phoenician warships after defeating them near Mycale[110]; and on the same day he enjoyed comparable success in a land battle. After capturing the enemy's ships, he immediately conducted a seaborne infantry landing and shattered a large force of barbarians in one hammer-blow. He gained a huge amount of plunder through this victory. Because of the harshness of Athenian control, some of the Aegean islands were in open rebellion; Cimon strengthened ties with those who were cooperative, and compelled the alienated to resume their obligations.[111]

He evacuated the island of Scyros,[112] which at that time was populated by the Dolopians,[113] as a consequence of their obstinate defiance; he ejected the original inhabitants from the city and the island and distributed the vacant lands to Athenian citizens. He subdued the Thasians[114]—who had relied on their money for leverage—merely by showing his face. Cimon's share of the plunder

---

[108] A river that marked the boundary between Macedonia and Thrace. The battle referred to took place in 476 B.C.
[109] This town was located near the mouth of the Strymon.
[110] Mycale was in Lydia, and the battle referred to took place in 479 B.C. Cimon was not involved in it, however; Nepos confuses this battle with a different one fought near Mycale in 466 B.C.
[111] *Bene animatas confirmavit, alienatas ad officium redire coegit.*
[112] An Aegean island that is part of the Sporades archipelago.
[113] Dolopia is a mountainous district north of Aetolia.
[114] Thasos is an island in the northern Aegean Sea. It produced good wine and had reserves of marble and precious metals.

financed the strengthening of the part of the Athenian Acropolis that lies to the south.¹¹⁵

3. As a result of these achievements he rose to become the most important figure in the state. He aroused the same antagonism as his father and other major statesmen of Athens had received before him: after a potsherd vote (which they call *ostrakismon*), he was expelled from the city for a period of ten years.¹¹⁶ Yet the Athenians came to regret this verdict sooner than Cimon himself did; for after he stepped aside with an unbroken spirit in the face of the ungrateful citizenry's malice, the Lacedaemonians initiated war against the Athenians, and there was a sudden necessity for Cimon's celebrated military skills. Thus he was called back four years after he had been sent into exile. Because of the guest relationship he enjoyed with the Lacedaemonians, and believing it preferable to deal with the Spartans directly, he proceeded to see them on his own accord, and concluded peace between these two very powerful city-states. Not long after this he was sent to Cyprus as commander of two hundred ships; and after he subdued the major part of the island, he contracted a disease and expired in the town of Citium.¹¹⁷

4. In peacetime as well as in war, the Athenians felt his loss for a long time. Although he had gardens and land in many different places, he was so generous that he never hired a custodian to safeguard his fruits, so that no one wanting to enjoy the products

---

¹¹⁵ *His ex manubiis arx Athenarum, qua ad meridiem vergit, est ornata.* The word *manubia* means the general's share of the plunder. Aulus Gellius (*Noct. Attic.* XIII.25) devotes several interesting pages to the etymology of this word, and how it differs from the standard word *praeda* (spoils). *Praeda*, he says, signifies the actual booty itself taken in war, while *manubia* is defined as the cash proceeds raised from the auction of such plunder by a Roman quaestor.

¹¹⁶ His banishment occurred in 461 B.C.

¹¹⁷ Citium was located on the southern coast of Cyprus.

of his land would be prevented from doing so. Attendants[118] accompanied him on foot with money; and someone needing financial help would receive what he could give on the spot, lest some postponement be interpreted as a denial. Many times, when he saw someone who had suffered the vagaries of Fortune and was inadequately clothed, he gave him his own cloak.

    A meal of such size was prepared for him on a daily basis that he could invite to his table anyone in the forum he saw fit to call; and he maintained this practice every day. No one needing his confidence, his personal efforts, or his monetary intervention made their pleas on deaf ears. There were many whom he made wealthy; and he handled the funeral arrangements of a good many deceased who were so impoverished that they had left nothing to provide for their own burials. As this was his way of doing things, one can hardly be surprised that his life remained unperturbed, and his death was bitterly mourned.

---

[118] An interesting word is used here: *pedissequus*, literally a "follower on foot."

Frontispiece of a creative 1662 German edition of Nepos, printed in Nuremburg. The historical names are arranged in formation as armed men, or edged weapons.

VI. Lysander [?—395 B.C.]

1. Lysander the Lacedaemonian left an impressive legacy, one acquired more by fortuitous circumstance than by virtue. It is clear that he stopped the Athenians, who had been waging war against the Peloponnesians for twenty-six years.[119] How this happened is not difficult to understand, for it was not his army's bravery, but the ineptitude of his enemies, that brought about this result. His opponents paid no attention to their leaders' orders; after they left their ships, they wandered aimlessly about the countryside before being reduced to impotence by their enemies. The final result was that the Athenians capitulated to the Lacedaemonians.

Lysander prided himself on that victory. Although before this he had always been impetuous and conniving, he now indulged himself to such an extent that the Lacedaemonians became the focus of hatred by the whole of Greece as a result of his behavior. For although they had professed that their reason for waging war was to shatter the dominance of the Athenians, once Lysander had captured the enemy fleet at the Battle of Aegospotami,[120] he labored single-mindedly to bring all the Greek city-states under his power while maintaining the charade that he was acting in the Lacedaemonians' interests. He everywhere purged those who

---

[119] Referring to the Peloponnesian War between Athens and Sparta.
[120] This naval action took place in the Hellespont 405 B.C. and was the last major engagement of the Peloponnesian War. Nepos uses the phrase *Aegos flumen* to identify the location, due to a stream ("Goat's River") that empties into the Hellespont.

sympathized with the Athenians, and appointed ten men in each city-state on whom he conferred wide-ranging powers and the responsibility for civil and military matters. No one was considered for these positions unless he had a relationship of hospitality with Lysander, or unless he affirmed his loyalty to him.

2. Once he had set up the power of the decemvirs in every city, everything was carried out according to his wishes. We will provide an example of his viciousness and perfidy with the single anecdote that follows, lest we fatigue readers with the repetition of many such stories. When he was returning to Greece after his victory in Asia,[121] he paused to visit Thasos, because that city had shown particular loyalty to the Athenians. Despite the fact that those who have been the most resolute enemies quite often become the firmest of friends, Lysander had a seething desire to destroy the city. He was aware, however, that unless he kept his intention hidden, the Thasians would evacuate the city and secure their possessions...[122]

---

[121] In 404 B.C.
[122] There is lacuna in the text here.

A 1553 woodcut depicting Lysander

3. The Spartans therefore dissolved the authority of the decemvirs that Lysander had taken such pains to organize. Burning with indignation at this decision, he conspired to overthrow the rule of the Lacedaemonian kings. Without the assistance of the gods, Lysander knew he would have no chance of carrying out this enterprise, since the Lacedaemonians were in the habit of referring all important questions to the oracles. He first made an effort to bribe the oracle at Delphi; when this was unsuccessful, he tried the same thing with the Dodona oracle. His approach there was also rebuffed. Then, thinking he could more easily corrupt the Africans, Lysander claimed he had undertaken a religious obligation for the sake of Jupiter Hammon.[123]

The priests of Jupiter promptly disabused him of his notions once he arrived in Africa, however. Not only did they prove to be incorruptible, but they even sent envoys to Lacedaemon accusing Lysander of trying to bribe the temple's priests. An indictment was filed against him for this crime, but the jury's verdict declared him not guilty. He was then sent to the Orchomenians as an advisor, but was killed by the Thebans near Haliartus.[124]

A speech discovered in his house after his death demonstrated the veracity of the accusations against him. It recommended that the Spartans dissolve the royal power and select a leader from the citizenry who would have the ability to wage war; but it was written in such a way to appear that its proposals were endorsed by the gods. He had no doubt he could obtain this divine "suggestion" by making use of his money. The speech is supposed to have been written for him by Cleon of Halicarnassus.

4. At this point I cannot let pass the opportunity to relate a certain action of Pharnabazus, one of the Persian king's satraps. In his position as wartime naval commander Lysander had left an

---

[123] Roman name of an African deity for whom a temple was constructed in Libya.
[124] Orchomenus and Haliartus were towns in Boeotia.

extended trail of greed and malice, and suspected that word of these incidents had been conveyed to his countrymen back home. He asked Pharnabazus to provide him with an affidavit he could give to the ephors; the document would state that he had waged war and dealt with his allies in an appropriately moral fashion. He wanted the Persian to provide a detailed account along these lines, knowing that his testimony would carry a great deal of credibility with the ephors. Pharnabazus gave him an expansive assurance to this effect; he penned an impressive volume[125] in many words that lavished on Lysander the highest praise.

This volume Lysander read and endorsed. While it was being prepared for sealing, another volume of equal bulk—so similar that it appeared to be exactly the same as the first—was promptly sealed and swapped for the other. The substituted scroll offered an exhaustive chronicle of the Spartan's perfidy and greed. When Lysander returned home and tried to submit his own version of events before the high tribunal, he provided as an evidentiary affidavit the written account Pharnabazus had given him. The ephors studied the volume outside of Lysander's presence; after reconvening, they then gave it to him to examine. So it was that he had unwittingly become his own prosecutor.

---

[125] I.e., scroll.

Lysander

VII. Alcibiades [C. 450 B.C.—404 B.C.]

1. Alcibiades the Athenian, the son of Clinias.[126] In this man it seems proven just what things nature was capable of; for all writers who produced accounts of his life confirm that there was no one who bested him either in vices or virtues. He came from a noble lineage in the most distinguished of city-states, and was by far the handsomest man of his era. He was proficient in every area of endeavor and excelled in good judgment; he was a gifted commander on both land and sea; and his eloquence put him in the highest rank of orators, since the style and content of his speeches were so compelling that no one could fail to be convinced by them. He was wealthy; when the situation required, he could work with great intensity. He had endurance; he was generous, and no less dashing in his personal life than he was as a public figure. He was affable and charming, capable of responding skillfully to the needs of the moment; yet by the same token, as soon as he slowed down and lacked a challenge to engage his faculties, his immoderation, dissolute habits, proclivity for sexual indulgence, and indiscipline became so pronounced that all men were astonished at how such a variegated and incongruous nature could be united in one person.

2. He was educated in the house of Pericles—for he is said to have been his stepson—and received instruction from Socrates. His father-in-law was Hipponicus, the wealthiest man in the entire

---

[126] Clinias perished in 447 B.C. in the Battle of Coronea during the First Peloponnesian War.

Greek-speaking world. If he had wished to construct his own ideal life, he could hardly have envisioned more favorable conditions or such incomparable opportunities as those provided to him by nature and fortune. As an adolescent he was loved by many according to Greek custom; among them was Socrates, a fact that Plato mentions in his dialogue *Symposium*. Plato depicts Alcibiades as saying that he had spent the night with Socrates, and arose precisely as a son should arise from his father's bed. After he had risen to maturity he took a good many lovers; and in these affairs, as far as is possible with such offensive customs, he displayed a considerable degree of refinement and humor. Anecdotes describing these qualities would be worthy of our attention if I did not have more pressing and relevant matters to discuss.

3. During the Peloponnesian War the Athenians declared war on Syracuse[127] as a result of his counsel and authority. He himself was chosen to be the wartime leader, and was provided with two colleagues, Nicias and Lamachus. One night, while the military force was being equipped and before the fleet left, all the busts of Hermes in the streets of Athens were toppled over except one. The bust that remained intact was located before the door of Andocides; and from that point forward it was called the "Mercury of Andocides." Since it was clear that the incident could not have taken place without the coordination of many participants, and that it was more of a political message than a private matter, a pervasive fear spread among the people that some shadowy force aligned against the state might strip them of their freedom.

---

[127] This took place in 415 B.C.

A 1553 woodcut of Alcibiades

The hand of Alcibiades was suspected as being behind this affair, because he was known to have more influence and power than an ordinary citizen. He had won the loyalty of many men through his generosity, and through the court system had made many others financially obligated to him. The inevitable result was that whenever he made a public appearance, all eyes were fixed firmly on him, and no one else in the state was treated as his equal. Thus Alcibiades became the embodiment not only of their highest hopes, but also of their deepest fears; for they knew he had the ability to perform a great deal of good, as well as inflict catastrophic harm. A vague cloud of scandal hovered about him as well, for he was alleged to conduct mystery ceremonies[128] in his house; this sort of practice was considered impious according to Athenian custom. It was believed that his involvement in these cultic ceremonies sprang not from genuine religious sentiment, but rather from a darker conspiratorial intent.

4. In fact this was the accusation leveled against him by his political enemies in the Athenian assembly. But the time had arrived for proceeding with the war. Cognizant of this fact, and well acquainted with the habits of his fellow Athenians, Alcibiades demanded that if his countrymen wanted to bring charges against him, they should hold the inquiry while he was still there, instead of making accusations in bad faith while he was absent. Since they knew he was invulnerable, his enemies for the time being preferred to hold their tongues and wait until he had left Athens, so that they could assail him in his absence. And this is precisely what happened. Once they knew he had reached the island of Sicily, they indicted him *in absentia* for blaspheming the traditional religious ceremonies.

For this reason an envoy was dispatched to him from the magistracy to return home and answer the charge. Although his command

---

[128] These secret religious rites or organizations were a feature of pagan antiquity. Only the initiated were allowed to take part in them.

had been competently run and bore favorable expectations, Alcibiades did not wish to ignore the directive and so boarded the trireme that had been sent to recall him. This vessel brought him to Thurii[129] in Italy. Brooding there on the excessive license of his fellow Athenians and their malice towards prominent men, he concluded it would be much wiser to evade the impending tempest. So he slipped away from his escort and headed first to Elis, then to Thebes. Once he heard, however, that he had been sentenced to death, that his estate had been confiscated, that the Athenian public had ordered the Eumolpidae[130] to mark him with a religious curse, and that the text of this condemnation had been carved on a publicly displayed stone pillar to solemnize the verdict, he decided to move to Lacedaemon.

---

[129] A town in *Magna Graecia* (southern Italy).
[130] The Eumolpidae were priests who conducted the Eleusinian mystery rites (i.e., the cults of Demeter and Persephone). They were named after their mythical founder, a priest named Eumolpus.

Alcibiades

There he waged war against his political enemies rather than against his country (a distinction he was careful to make): for his antagonists in Athens were in fact the enemies of their own country. Even though they knew Alcibiades could be of great value to the state, they had engineered his expulsion from Athens more on account of their personal malice than from any considerations of public good. Through his recommendation, the Lacedaemonians embraced the king of Persia in friendship and consolidated their position at Decelea[131] in Attica by stationing a permanent detachment of soldiers there. This move had the effect of imposing a blockade on Athens. His diplomatic efforts also detached the Ionian region from the Athenian sphere of influence; and as a direct result of this, the tide of war began to shift in Sparta's favor.

5. Nevertheless Alcibiades's cooperation with the Spartans did not result in their embracing him in friendship: it instead made them keep a nervous distance from him. Well aware of the outstanding judgment of that shrewdest of men in all things, they were apprehensive that affection for his homeland would eventually lead him to abandon Sparta and make peace with his fellow Athenians. They therefore began to look for a chance to have him killed. This intention could not long be hidden from Alcibiades; his shrewdness was such that he could not be duped, especially when he sensed the need for wariness. So he made his way to Tissaphernes,[132] one of the prefects of king Darius, and gained the king's close friendship. Observing that Athenian influence was in decline after the disasters that had happened in Sicily, and that the power of the Lacedaemonians was steadily rising, he first began negotiations using intermediaries with Pisander, the commander of an army at Samos.

To him Alcibiades made mention of a return to Athens. Pisander and he were of the same mind; he was hostile to popular

---

[131] A town in north Attica.
[132] Persian soldier and statesman (445 B.C.—395 B.C.).

sovereignty and sympathetic to the aristocrats. Yet nothing came of these talks, and Alcibiades was first taken in by the army through Thrasybulus, the son of Lycus, and appointed to a command on Samos. With the express endorsement of Theramenes, he was later rehabilitated by popular vote and in his absence given co-equal authority with Thrasybulus and Theramenes. Such a reversal of fortune took place while these men were in charge that the Lacedaemonians, who only a short while earlier were preening as victors, were now frantically begging for a peace agreement. They had been routed in five land battles and in three naval engagements where two hundred triremes were lost; these ships had been seized and taken away by Sparta's enemy.

Coordinating his actions with his associates, Alcibiades took possession of Ionia, the Hellespont, and many other Greek cities scattered along the Asiatic coast. A fair number of these cities, including Byzantium, were forcibly seized; but an equal number had been persuaded to become allies through employment of a clemency policy towards captives. Overloaded with plunder and with an army now wealthy, they returned to Athens[133] with these impressive accomplishments to their credit.

6. The entire city descended on the Piraeus for their arrival. Such was everyone's suspense in wanting to see Alcibiades that the common people flocked eagerly to his trireme just as if he had arrived alone. For the public clung to the belief that their earlier misfortunes and their current favorable circumstances were linked to him; thus they themselves, because they had forced into exile such an outstanding statesman, accepted responsibility for the loss of Sicily and other Spartan victories. This thinking was not entirely without a foundation in truth. For once Alcibiades had assumed command of the army, the enemy was unable to hold their own against Athens on either land or sea.

Although Thrasybulus and Theramenes were his co-equal commanders and had arrived at the Piraeus with him at the same time, as soon as Alcibiades stepped off his ship he was the man

---

[133] In 407 B.C.

everyone escorted; the people gifted him golden crowns and ribbons, something that had never before been done for anyone except the victors at Olympia. Mindful of the residual bitterness from past times, he wept as he received this sincere display of goodwill from his fellow citizens.

The Athenian assembly was convened once Alcibiades had arrived in the city. The address he delivered was so moving that there was no one so intractable who did not grieve at his ordeal and express rage at those who had engineered his expulsion. It was as if an entirely different group of people had denounced him for sacrilege, rather than those who were now crying in the assembly.[134] He received restitution from public funds for his confiscated property. The Eumolpidae were forced to lift the curse they had placed on him earlier, and the stone pillars on which the curse had been carved were hurled into the sea.

7. Alcibiades's happiness was not to last for long. Once all the honors had been awarded to him, and every domestic and military matter was placed in his hands to be resolved according to his exclusive judgment, and once he asked to be given his two colleagues Thrasybulus and Adimantus and the request was not refused, he departed with a fleet for Asia. But because the final results at Cyme[135] had not matched his original intentions, he again came under a cloud of disapproval, for they had come to believe he was capable of doing anything. The result of this perception was that they saddled him with the blame for everything that went wrong, saying that he had been either negligent or malicious. So it was the case here. They accused him of not making an effort to capture Cyme because the king had bribed him. Thus I am convinced that

---

[134] Nepos's scorn at the Athenian leadership's hypocrisy is undisguised here.

[135] A town in Mysia in Asia Minor. Nepos's account of these events is somewhat confused. Alcibiades unjustly plundered Cyme, an Athenian ally. While this was happening, he advised a colleague, Antiochus, not to engage Lysander in a naval battle. Antiochus did, and was defeated. Blame for the entire debacle was placed on Alcibiades.

their inflated opinion of his talents and martial prowess became for him an unmitigated evil. For he was feared no less than he was esteemed; and his countrymen worried that, once lifted high by good fortune and immense power, he would begin to covet tyrannical authority.

Frontispiece of a 1756 edition of Nepos

The consequence of these sentiments was that they revoked his appointment during his absence and chose another commander to replace him. Once he learned of this decision, he no longer had any desire to return home; instead he moved to Pactye[136] and strengthened three fortresses, Orni, Bizanthe and Neontichos. Believing it was more honorable to enrich himself by attacking barbarians than Greeks, he formed a band of soldiers and became the first representative of a Greek state to invade Thrace. The result of this incursion was the elevation of Alcibiades's fame and riches; he also earned the lasting friendship of some of the Thracian kings.

8. Nevertheless, he was unable to walk away from the genuine affection he retained for his homeland. When the Athenian general Philocles brought his fleet to Aegospotamoi, and the nearby Spartan commander Lysander was doing everything in his power to drag out the war, since the Persian king was funneling money to the Spartans while the exhausted Athenians had nothing except their weapons and ships, Alcibiades came to the Athenian army and initiated a direct appeal to the common soldiers. He promised them that, if they wished, he would force Lysander either to fight or to make peace. He assured them that the Lacedaemonians had no desire to risk a naval engagement, since their land forces were stronger than their navy. It would be a simple matter, Alcibiades stated, for him to persuade the Thracian king Seuthes to expel Lysander from the land; and once this was done, Lysander would either have to fight Athens at sea or bring the war to a conclusion.

Although Philocles knew that Alcibiades was speaking the truth, he did not want to cooperate with the idea. He knew very well that, if Alcibiades were again rehabilitated,[137] he himself would be marginalized in the army. If Alcibiades's strategy met

---

[136] A town on the coast of Thrace.
[137] I.e., brought back into favor (using the ablative absolute *Alcibiade recepto*).

with success, his involvement in it would go largely unnoticed; but if things went badly, he alone would be saddled with the blame. When he left him, Alcibiades said, "Since you want your country to fail, I will give you this warning: do not place your naval camp near the enemy. There is a danger that your men's indiscipline will provide Lysander the opening needed to destroy your army." He was not wrong about this observation. For when Lysander discovered through spies that a large group of Athenian soldiers had gone ashore to search for plunder—thus leaving the ships almost unmanned—he did not fail to seize the opportunity for action. He wound up the entire war in one stroke.

9. But once the Athenians were defeated, Alcibiades believed he was no longer safe in the place where he was; he traveled deep into Thrace and beyond the Propontis,[138] hoping that his notoriety could more easily be hidden there. This was a delusion.[139] For as soon as the Thracians learned he had arrived there with a large amount of money, they ambushed him and ran off with everything he had; they were unable, however, to take Alcibiades himself hostage. Realizing that nowhere in Greece was safe for him because of the long reach of Lacedaemonian power, he crossed into Asia to live under the protection of Pharnabazus. This Persian ruler was so impressed with Alcibiades's charisma that he made him his closest friend. Pharnabazus gifted him Grynium, a fortress in Phrygia,[140] from which he took fifty talents annually in revenue.

But Alcibiades was not satisfied with this state of affairs; neither could he accept the fact that a defeated Athens was now subservient to the Lacedaemonians. Thus he could think of nothing else than the liberation of his homeland. But he understood that nothing could be accomplished without the Persian king; and for this reason he desired to win him over as an ally. Alcibiades

---

[138] Now called the Sea of Marmara.
[139] Nepos uses one word for this sentence: *Falso*.
[140] The region of Phrygia was located in the west-central part of Anatolia (Asia Minor).

had no doubt that, if he were just given the chance for a personal introduction, he could easily accomplish this goal. For he was aware that the king's brother Cyrus was making covert arrangements for armed action[141] with Lacedaemonian help; and Alcibiades thought that if he could disclose this information, he would make himself highly favored.

10. While Alcibiades was plotting these moves and pleading for Pharnabazus to send him to the king, Critias and the other Athenian tyrants dispatched reliable men to Asia.[142] They let Lysander know that unless he destroyed Alcibiades, none of the issues he had decided at Athens would remain settled. Thus, if he wanted his decisions to be assured of permanence, he needed to pursue Alcibiades relentlessly. The Laconian was thrown off balance by these developments, and thought it would be better to deal with Pharnabazus. He made it clear he would abrogate the settlement that the king had reached with the Lacedaemonians unless Pharnabazus turned over Alcibiades alive or dead. The Persian satrap was unable to take this kind of pressure: rather than see the king's power reduced, he chose to violate the accepted law of clemency.

Accordingly, Pharnabazus dispatched Susamithres and Bagaeus on a mission to assassinate Alcibiades while he was in Phrygia preparing to visit the king. These legates secretly put out word to those living near Alcibiades's residence that they should murder him. None of these locals had the courage to draw a weapon against him. Instead, in order to achieve by fire that which they did not have the courage to achieve by the sword, they piled wood at night around the house where he slept and set it ablaze.[143]

Alcibiades was awakened by the sound of the flames. Although his sword had been taken from him, he armed himself with

---

[141] Meaning armed action against Artaxerxes.
[142] This "junta" of thirty men was installed in Athens by the victorious Lysander in 404 B.C.
[143] The scorn in Nepos's words comes through very clearly.

his friend's short knife; for there was a close comrade from Arcadia also staying there who never left his side. He ordered his companion to help him, then seized all the clothing that was close by. Once these were thrown down to smother the fire, Alcibiades forced his way through the flames. When the barbarians saw that he had made his way out of the burning house, they threw javelins at him from a distance and killed him. They then brought his severed head to Pharnabazus. But a woman who used to live with him wrapped his remains with one of her garments and cremated his body in the blazing edifice—a fire that had been intended to extinguish his natural life. So did Alcibiades perish at the age of about forty years.[144]

11. Many writers have brought his legacy into disrepute. Three distinguished historians, however, have conferred on him the highest praise: Thucydides, who was one of his contemporaries; Theopompus,[145] who was born some time later; and Timaeus.[146] These last two excessively hostile[147] writers apparently share the same sentiments in speaking favorably about Alcibiades, for I have relied on their narratives for what I have written above. The following verdict on Alcibiades may also be rendered. Although he was born in Athens, that most celebrated of cities, he outdid all his contemporaries in the grandeur and illustriousness of his life. After he had been expelled from Athens and went to Thebes, he accommodated himself so well to Theban culture that no one could match him in capacity for work or physical strength—for in general the Boeotians are more inclined to favor physical strength than intellectual ability.

---

[144] His age was probably closer to forty-six.
[145] (c. 378 B.C.—c. 300 B.C.). A historian from Chios who continued the history of Thucydides.
[146] (c. 350 B.C.—c. 254 B.C.). A Sicilian historian who wrote a history of his island. Both Theopompus's and Timaeus's works are lost.
[147] The precise word used here is *maledicentissimi*: i.e., those inordinately fond of speaking ill of others.

This same man so dedicated himself to ascetic severity when he was with the Lacedaemonians—whose customs place the highest value on the ability to tolerate hardship—that he excelled them in his parsimony with food and life's refinements. When he was with the Thracians, a people devoted to excessive drinking and sexual profligacy, he bested them too in these wanton activities. When he lived among the Persians, where the greatest merit is earned by hunting bravely and living sumptuously, he so mastered these practices that even they held him in the highest admiration. It was through the use of these innate abilities that, no matter where he found himself, he occupied the highest rank among men and was regarded with the sincerest affection. But about his life, we have said enough. Let us continue with our remaining profiles.

VIII. Thrasybulus [C. 440 B.C.—388 B.C.]

1. Thrasybulus the Athenian, the son of Lycus. If masculine virtue were to be evaluated by itself without considering the intervention of fortune, I would not hesitate to place Thrasybulus before all other men. The following is certain: I rank no one above him in integrity, perseverance, greatness of soul,[148] and in devotion to country. For although many have wanted to free their homeland from the clutches of one tyrant, and a few have been able to do so, he was successful in taking his country from subservience to liberation when it was under the domination of thirty tyrants. And although no one was his equal in the virtues I have just listed, for some reason many other names have achieved more notoriety than his. During the Peloponnesian War he was able to handle many crises without Alcibiades; but Alcibiades could do nothing without him. Yet Alcibiades, through his natural charisma, always reaped the benefits himself.

To be sure, commanders and soldiers share all such rewards with each other and with fortune; for once the roar of battle commences, the outcome of the fighting depends on strength and number. Thus the common soldier rightly asserts, no less than his commander, a share of the credit for victory. Fortune claims an even bigger share; she may, in these situations, justifiably assert that her contribution to the outcome was more decisive than the skill of the general. The truly magnificent action described below,

---

[148] Nepos uses the same *magnitudo animi* (greatness of soul) that Cicero speaks of in *On Duties*.

however, came about through the effort of Thrasybulus alone. For thirty tyrants installed by the Lacedaemonians held Athens in a state of vassalage.[149] They expelled a great number of citizens whom fortune had spared from the war's carnage, and executed some others. They seized the property of many Athenians and divided it up among themselves. Thrasybulus was not only the first man to confront the tyrants openly: he was at first the *only man* to do so.

2. When he fled to Phyle,[150] a very secure fortress in Attica, he had not more than thirty compatriots with him. This was the beginning of a rebirth for the Attic people, a flaming beacon of liberty for an illustrious state. In his isolated condition, he was at first looked upon with derision by the tyrants and even by his own men—and yet, indeed, it was this contempt that eventually led to their downfall. For their scorn initially provided him a measure of security. The tyrants put little effort into pursuing him; and their disregard made his band stronger by giving Thrasybulus the time needed to prepare for conflict. Thus every man should be mindful of the maxim that *in war nothing should be treated with disdain;*[151] and it is most assuredly true that *the mother of a fearful man has no reason to shed tears.*[152]

---

[149] When the Spartans defeated Athens in the Peloponnesian War in 404 B.C., they installed a government of thirty oligarchs that would carry out Spartan policies.

[150] Phyle was located about eighteen miles north of Athens.

[151] *Nihil in bello oportere contemni.*

[152] *Neque sine causa dici matrem timidi flere non solere.* The fearful man, neglecting nothing, is always on his guard, and this will preserve his safety. He gives his mother no cause for panic.

A 1553 woodcut depicting Thrasybulus

Nevertheless Thrasybulus's influence did not extend as far as he wished; for even in that era people showed more courage in speaking about liberty than in taking action to win it. From Phyle he crossed into Piraeus and fortified Munychia.[153] The tyrants twice mounted an assault on this place, but were brutally defeated and forced back to the city, losing their weapons and logistical supplies in the process. Thrasybulus displayed no less prudence than valor. He prohibited atrocities from being committed against prisoners of war, believing that citizens should refrain from violence against fellow citizens. No one was injured unless he chose to attack first. No man who had fallen was robbed of his clothing; he laid his hands on nothing except the weapons he needed, and whatever he could use in the way of food. Critias, the leader of the tyrants, was slain in a second battle while fighting courageously against Thrasybulus himself.

3. After the death of Critias, the Lacedaemonian king Pausanias arrived on the scene to help the people of Attica. He negotiated peace between Thrasybulus and the men who held the city on the following conditions: (1) that no one should be subjected to banishment or confiscation of property except for the thirty tyrants and ten others installed later who had practiced the same cruelty as their antecedents; and (2) that the leadership of the republic should be handed back to the Athenian people. Another of Thrasybulus's admirable rulings was that when hostilities ended and he held the reins of power in the state, he enacted a law stating that there would be no accusations or retribution with regard to events that had taken place in the past. They called this the "law of reconciliation."[154] He made sure not only that this decree was passed, but that it was vigorously applied. For any time one of those who had been in exile with him tried to execute those

---

[153] Munychia was a hill located in Piraeus. It is today a fashionable neighborhood. The Battle of Munychia took place in 404 or 403 B.C. between the forces of the Thirty Tyrants and the Athenians who had been exiled by them.
[154] The word is *oblivio*, literally "forgetfulness."

who had been formally granted amnesty, he put a stop to it. What he had promised, he honored.

4. In grateful acknowledgment of his public service, he was awarded an honorary crown by the Athenian people made from two olive branches. Rather than having been extorted by force, this honor was bestowed on him by the love of his people. It was attended by no jealousy, and was surrounded by great glory. Pittacus, who was counted among the famed "Seven Sages," made this point best when the citizens of Mytilene tried to give him many thousands of acres of land as a gift.[155] He demurred, saying, "I beg you, do not give me something that will arouse the envy of many, and that even more will covet. From what you offer I do not want more than one hundred acres. Let these be evidence of my sense of restraint, and of your sincerity."

Small gifts are enduring, while opulent ones are usually not special. Thrasybulus was quite satisfied with that crown; he did not ask for anything else and believed he had been granted an honor that no other man could claim. Later in his life, he was in command of a fleet that put ashore at Cilicia, and his camp was not guarded with adequate vigilance. Barbarians from a nearby town launched a night assault, and he was slain in his tent.[156]

---

[155] Pittacus (c. 640 B.C.—568 B.C.) was a military commander from Mytilene (in the island of Lesbos) and one of the so-called "Seven Sages of Greece."

[156] He was actually killed in the southern Asia Minor region of Pamphylia, which lies between Lycia and Cilicia.

IX. Conon [C. 444 B.C.—C. 394 B.C.]

1. Conon the Athenian entered politics during the Peloponnesian War, an event in which he played a major role. He served as a general in the infantry, and as a naval commander he had some great achievements to his credit. For these contributions to the war effort, he was granted a special honor: he was given sole management responsibility for all the islands. While serving in this capacity, he took charge of Pherae,[157] a Lacedaemonian colony. He was also a general at the end of the Peloponnesian War, when the Athenian forces were routed by Lysander at Aegospotamoi. He was not present at this incident, however, and as a result it was handled incompetently; for he was an industrious commander and quite experienced in military affairs. No one who was a contemporary of these events had any doubt that the Athenians would never have endured this shattering defeat had Conon been there.

2. Once disaster struck and he heard that his country was being blockaded, he sought to find a place where he could help his fellow countrymen, rather than a place where he could live in safety. He thus made his way to Pharnabazus,[158] the satrap[159] of Ionia and Lydia as well as the king's son-in-law and kinsman; through considerable effort and by running great risks, Conon made him a valued ally. When the Lacedaemonians defeated the Athenians, they did not honor the terms of the agreement they had made with

---

[157] A town in Messenia, a region of the Peloponnesus.
[158] This was in 398 B.C.
[159] He was the satrap of Phrygia; the satrap of Ionia and Lydia was Tissaphernes.

Artaxerxes; they sent Agesilaus to Asia to incite conflict at the behest of Tissaphernes. This latter individual was a close companion of Artaxerxes who had renounced his loyalty to the king and thrown in his lot with the Lacedaemonians.

In theory Pharnabazus was the military commander opposing Agesilaus, but in fact Conon was in charge of the army and it was he who issued all the directives. He seriously impeded the progress of that accomplished commander Agesilaus and blocked his plans on many occasions; and it is generally agreed that had Conon not been present, Agesilaus would have captured from the king all of Asia as far as the Taurus.[160] After Agesilaus had been recalled home by his fellow citizens when the Boeotians and Athenians initiated hostilities against Sparta, Conon continued without interruption his dealings with the king's subordinates and proved to be an invaluable ally.

3. While Tissaphernes had renounced his fealty to the king, this was not as apparent to Artaxerxes as it was to others. Since he continued to perform many useful tasks for his sovereign, he still had Artaxerxes's ear even after abandoning his official position. It is hardly surprising that the king found it difficult to believe in Tissaphernes's defection; for Artaxerxes knew that it was Tissaphernes's assistance that had allowed him to prevail over his brother Cyrus. Conon was sent to the king by Pharnabazus for the purpose of accusing Tissaphernes. According to Persian custom, after Conon arrived at the king's court, he first visited the chiliarch[161] Tithraustes, who held the secondary power after the king. Conon told him that he wanted to speak to the king. No one, it should be noted, is accorded such a privilege without following this protocol.

---

[160] The Taurus Mountains in Asia Minor.
[161] *Chiliarchus* is a Latin term imported from Greek, and means an officer commanding a force of one thousand men. Here it means the commander of the king's personal bodyguard. This office carried diplomatic as well as security responsibilities.

The chiliarch responded, "There is no problem with what you ask. But do you think the best way to present your request is in person, or with a written petition? For if you see the king in person, you are required to make a personal show of homage, a ritual the Greeks call *proskynesis*.[162] If you find this intolerable, you may present what you wish through me with no less effectiveness, once you have informed me of your purpose." Conon responded, "It is not intolerable for me to pay whatever respect is required to the king. But I fear receiving some reproach from my own people if, coming as I do from a land used to holding power over other nations, I should prefer the ritual of barbarians over the customs of my own people." He therefore composed and submitted a written petition.

4. Once the king found out what was going on, he was so swayed by Conon's influence that he ordered Tissaphernes to be branded an enemy. He authorized Conon to commence military action against the Lacedaemonians, and allowed him to choose whomever he wished to handle payroll matters. Conon said that the choice for war was not one he could make; it was something for the king to decide, as he was best informed of his people's interests. He suggested, however, that the king should give this responsibility to Pharnabazus. After receiving some expensive gifts, Conon was sent to the coast in order to enlist warships from the Cypriots, Phoenicians, and other sea-going nations; he was also tasked with assembling a fleet suitable for making the sea safe in the following summer. Pharnabazus was assigned the job of helping Conon, as the latter had wished.

When news of this reached the Lacedaemonians, they took great pains to ready themselves; they believed that a more serious war loomed than if they had to confront the barbarians alone. For they knew that a strong leader would be capably directing the

---

[162] Προσκύνησις, or the traditional formality of prostrating oneself on the ground in the presence of an oriental monarch. This practice would have been particularly unpleasant to a democratically minded Athenian of Conon's era.

king's forces, and that they would be contending with an opponent whom they exceeded in neither skill nor resources. With this in mind they assembled a large fleet and left port with Pisander[163] in command of the expedition. Conon intercepted and smashed them near Cnidus in a huge battle; he captured many vessels and sank a number of them as well.[164] With this victory not only Athens was freed, but also the remainder of those city-states that were under the control of the Lacedaemonians. Conon went to his homeland with some of his ships and supervised the reconstruction of the walls (which had been demolished by Lysander) of both the Piraeus and Athens. To his fellow citizens he also donated a sum of money he had received from Pharnabazus in the amount of fifty talents.

---

[163] The brother-in-law of King Agesilaus.
[164] The Battle of Cnidus took place in 394 B.C. Cnidus was a coastal city in Caria in southern Asia Minor.

Conon

5. Yet the same fate befell Conon that was visited on other men, in that he was less prudent in times of good fortune than he was during times of hardship. Having routed the Peloponnesian fleet, and believing he had avenged his homeland's ill-treatment, he began to covet things that were impossible for him to achieve. These aspirations were nevertheless righteous and respectable, since he was aiming at increasing the influence of his own country over that of the Persian king. The naval engagement he had fought near Cnidus had accorded him great prestige not only with the barbarians, but also with all the Greek states; and secretly he began to prepare for the return of Ionia and Aeolia to Athenian control.

But his designs were insufficiently safeguarded. Tiribazus, who was in charge at Sardis,[165] asked Conon to come there; the pretext used was that he wanted to dispatch him on an important mission to the king. The Athenian complied with this request, but was tossed into prison as soon as he arrived and stayed there for a considerable time. While some authorities record that he was brought to the king and eventually perished, the historian Dinon,[166] who has a great deal of credibility on the subject of Persian history, relates that Conon escaped from custody. It is unclear, however, whether this occurred with Tiribazus's complicity or as a result of his ineptitude.

---

[165] A city in Lydia.
[166] He seems to have flourished around 360 B.C.—340 B.C. Only fragments of his work survive.

X. Dion [408 B.C.—354 B.C.]

1. Dion of Syracuse, the son of Hipparinus, came from a distinguished family and had connections with both tyrants who shared the name Dionysius. The elder Dionysius married Dion's sister Aristomache; with her he had two sons, Hipparinus and Nisaeus, as well as two daughters, Sophrosyne and Arete. He gave Sophrosyne in marriage to the son Dionysius (to whom he bequeathed his royal power). He gave his other daughter Arete to Dion.[167]

Besides this impressive affiliation and the noble reputation of his family's history, Dion had many intrinsic qualities of character: a mind that learned quickly, graciousness, and a suitability for high achievement. He carried himself with great dignity, something that recommends itself in no small way; and from his father he inherited significant wealth that the tyrant's gifts helped to augment. He was close to the elder Dionysius as much because of shared personal traits as because of their familial connection. For although he had an aversion to Dionysius's cruelty, his safety mattered to him because of their personal ties—and even more so for the sake of his own immediate relatives.

Dion carried out various tasks for the tyrant, who was usually receptive to his advice except in situations where a more compelling desire of Dionysius would intrude. All important diplomatic

---

[167] The elder Dionysius ruled Syracuse from 405 B.C. to 367 B.C. His son, the younger Dionysius, ruled from 367 B.C. to 356 B.C., the year in which he was overthrown. He returned to power in 346 B.C. but was again removed in 343 B.C., this time permanently.

missions were handled by Dion; and, assuming these tasks with diligence and carrying them out with integrity, he diminished, with his own benevolence, the taint of cruelty that stained the tyrant's name. When Dionysius sent him to Carthage, the Carthaginians so respected him that no Greek speaker was ever accorded comparable admiration.

2. These realities were certainly not lost on Dionysius. He knew to what extent Dion's prestige enhanced his own rule. The result of this was that he indulged him however he could, and valued Dion as if he were his own son. When word reached Sicily that Plato had arrived at Tarentum,[168] Dionysius could not deny the young man's desire to meet the philosopher, as Dion was consumed by a burning desire to hear Plato speak. The tyrant indulged Dion his wish and brought Plato to Syracuse with great fanfare. Dion so venerated and idolized the philosopher that he pledged himself entirely to Plato. For his part, Plato was no less enthralled with Dion. For although he was grievously betrayed by Dionysius—who ordered the Athenian philosopher to be sold into slavery—Plato still came back to Sicily, drawn once again by Dion's earnest request.

Meanwhile Dionysius had become sick. As the tyrant's condition deteriorated, Dion asked the physicians about his prognosis; at the same time he begged them not to hide the truth from him if Dionysius's state became even more precarious. Dion told them he wanted to talk with the declining Dionysius about the proper division of his kingdom; he believed that his sister's sons deserved a share of it, since they were the king's offspring. But the doctors did not preserve the confidentiality of Dion's words: they conveyed what he had said to Dionysius's son. The younger Dionysius was greatly agitated upon being told this; and in order to deprive Dion the chance to speak to the ailing ruler, he

---

[168] An ancient city located on the southern coast of Apulia in Italy, in what was then called Magna Graecia.

instructed the doctors to give his father a strong sedative. Once this tranquilizing agent was administered, the patient drifted off into a sleep that proved to be eternal.

3. Such was the genesis of the hatred between Dion and the younger Dionysius, and it would become augmented by various factors. Nevertheless for some time they seemingly remained on cordial terms. When Dion would not stop asking Dionysius to invite Plato from Athens and make use of his philosophy, Dionysius—who wanted to imitate his father in some way—finally agreed. At the same time he ordered the historian Philistus to return to Syracuse, a man who was just as ill-disposed to the Syracusan tyrant as he was to all tyrants. I have already discussed him in detail, however, in the book I published on the Greek historians. So completely did Plato win over the tyrant, and so powerful was the philosopher's eloquence, that he convinced Dionysius to abandon his tyrannical habits and give the Syracusans back their liberty. But Philistus's counsel discouraged Dionysius from implementing this plan, and the tyrant persisted in his old ways—only now he became even more severe.

4. Dionysius well knew that Dion was his superior in natural qualities of character, leadership ability, and in the devotion of the masses; and he feared that if Dion remained close to the throne, his competitor might be given some opportunity to unseat him. So he provided him a trireme in which he could go to Corinth, saying that he was doing this for their mutual benefit. Since they were suspicious of each other, he reasoned, each of them would constantly be looking for a chance to undermine the other. This move provoked a great deal of resentment and pervasive hostility against the tyrant. Dionysius dumped all of Dion's transferable belongings into ships and sent this cargo to him. He wanted the public to think not that he was motivated by animus against Dion, but that he was scrupulously looking out for his rival's well-being.

However, when the tyrant learned that Dion was preparing a force in the Peloponnesus to mount an expedition against him, he gave Dion's wife Arete away to another man in marriage, and made sure that his son was reared in such a way that permissiveness corrupted him with the most disgraceful impulses. For before the young man reached adulthood, he was induced to cavort with prostitutes, plied with rich foods and wine, and was never permitted to maintain his sobriety. Once his father Dion came back to his homeland, attendants were assigned to the boy to cure him of his former degenerate conduct; but the son was so unable to adapt himself to the new circumstances of his life that he leapt from the top of his house and was killed. But let me return to my narrative.

Dion

5. Once Dion landed in Corinth, Dionysius's former cavalry commander Heraclides (who had also been exiled) decided to take up residence there. The two of them began to plan a military operation, but their efforts produced little. Because tyrants had been in control for so many years, they were widely considered to be an immoveable force, and thus few could be persuaded to expose themselves to any danger. But Dion placed more faith in his revulsion for the Syracusan tyrant than on his material resources; and with the most surpassing courage, he set out with two vessels to attack a regime that had been in power for fifty years, a regime protected by five hundred warships, ten thousand cavalry, and one hundred thousand infantry.

And yet, in a feat that was greeted with astonishment by all nations, he so easily defeated the regime that he entered Syracuse on the third day after landing in Sicily. We may conclude from this that no realm is safe unless it is supported by goodwill.[169] Dionysius was not in Sicily at that time; believing that no one would advance on him without a large military force, he chose to wait for the enemy's fleet in Italy. He could not have been more wrong. For Dion, with those same people who had been under his adversary's power, dealt the king's prestige a fatal blow. He seized the entire part of Sicily that had been under Dionysius's control as well as Syracuse (except the citadel and island[170] belonging to the town). The expedition turned out so well that the tyrant agreed to a peace treaty with the following provisions: Dion would keep Sicily, Dionysius would have Italy, and Syracuse would be ceded to Apollocrates,[171] a man who enjoyed the complete confidence of Dionysius.

---

[169] *Ex quo intellegi potest nullum esse imperium tutum nisi benevolentia munitum.* I.e., the goodwill of the people is a ruler's best safeguard.
[170] There was a fortified island named Ortygia that constituted part of Syracuse.
[171] He was Dionysius's eldest son. He was forced to give up his holdings in 354 B.C.

6. Yet a stark reversal soon followed upon the heel of these unanticipated victories. For fortune, with her predictable inconstancy, conspired to overwhelm the man whom she had extolled only a short time before. She first demonstrated her power with regard to the son I mentioned above. For when Dion's wife—who had been given to another man—was returned to him, and he was making efforts to restore to virtue the son that had fallen into moral corruption, he was forced to endure that son's death, the most terrible blow possible for a parent. After this, antagonism began to grow between him and Heraclides, who assembled a faction to oppose Dion because he could not bring himself to concede the leadership position. He had just as much influence in the aristocracy as did Dion, and with their endorsement he was put in charge of the fleet. Dion kept control of the army.

This outcome was not agreeable to him. He voiced a certain Homeric verse from the poet's second book, the gist of which is that a republic with many leaders cannot be well-managed. But this remark triggered a great deal of antagonistic feeling against him, for it seemed to reveal a desire on his part to secure unchallenged power. He made no effort to mollify this hostility with a show of deference; he instead tried to sweep it aside using extreme measures. When Heraclides came to Syracuse, Dion made arrangements for his murder.

7. This deed struck great fear into the hearts of all. No man felt safe after this wanton killing. With his adversary now out of the picture, he became even more unrestrained in conduct. He distributed among his soldiers the property of those he knew were his foes. Once he had disbursed these proceeds—for his day-to-day costs had become excessive—he quickly found himself in need of money; but there was nothing he could readily confiscate except the property of his friends. The outcome of this policy was that, although he reconciled with the soldiers, he entirely alienated the upper classes. He was worn down by the stress of these events; and, unused to being denounced, he could not accept the enmity

of those who only a little while earlier had hoisted him to the skies with conspicuous flattery. Once Dion no longer had the support of the military, the general public more openly voiced its displeasure, and stood firm in its opinion that a tyrant would not be accepted.

8. He watched these problems fester but was incapable of resolving them. And he lived in growing apprehension of the potential outcome. A man named Callicrates, an Athenian citizen who had come with Dion to Sicily from the Peloponnesus, a man proficient in the ways of trickery and fraud, and bereft of any sense of morals or integrity, visited Dion and told him this: "You are in great danger because of the public's anger and the dissatisfaction of the army. There is only one way to fix this problem, and that is to order some of your own men to pretend to be your opposition. If you find the right man for this task, he will quickly learn what the masses are thinking and can then move against your adversaries, for your enemies will reveal their true feelings to someone who looks like a dissident."

Once this scheme was endorsed, Callicrates himself, now empowered by Dion's foolishness, agreed to take on the role of the spy. He searched for allies to help with Dion's assassination. He organized the regime's opposition figures and confirmed their loyalty with a pledge of support. Because many were involved in the conspiracy, it was exposed and brought to the attention of Dion's sister Aristomache and his wife Arete. These two terrified women then went to the man whom they feared was in danger. Dion assured them that Callicrates was not a subversive, but rather was acting under his orders. Nevertheless the women led Callicrates to the temple of Proserpina and made him swear that his scheme would pose no danger to Dion. This little ritual not only did nothing to deter the schemer, it motivated him to launch his ripening plot even sooner. For he feared that his plan would be exposed before he could set it in motion.

9. With this goal in mind, on the next religious festival, when Dion was avoiding a public appearance and reclining in an upper

room of his house, Callicrates handed over the more well-defended parts of the town to his partners in crime. He ringed Dion's residence with guards who could be trusted not to move away from the doors. He outfitted a trireme with soldiers and placed his brother Philostratus in charge of it, then ordered him to row the ship around the harbor as if he were training his oarsmen. Callicrates's thinking was that if fortune happened to scuttle his plans, he would still have a way of fleeing to safety.

From his men he picked out a few youths from Zacynthos[172] known for their great daring and martial qualities, and instructed them to approach Dion unarmed, so that they could appear to be meeting him for a conference. Because the men were already known, they were readily admitted; but once they crossed the threshold of his residence, they bolted the doors, broke into his chambers where he was lying in bed, and immobilized him. The commotion that resulted from this activity was great enough to be heard outside.

Here, as we have noted before, the bitter resentment that absolute power engenders, and the miserable life of those who would rather be feared than loved, was on display for all to see.[173] For if Dion's own bodyguards had been favorably inclined to

---

[172] An island in the Ionian Sea.

[173] Perhaps relevant here are the wise words of the Arabic political philosopher Ibn Zafar al-Siqilli (1104—1170), who addressed this point in his treatise *Consolation of the Ruler Amid the Hostility of His Subjects* (سلوان المطاع في عدوان الأتباع): "Subjects first shake their tongues and then their fists. Rulers cannot control their tongues unless they master their whole bodies, nor will sovereigns remain in power unless they can win the hearts of the masses. But these hearts will never cleave to a sovereign if he does not administer justice impartially..." See Kechichian, J.A. & Dekmejian, H., *The Just Prince: A Manual of Leadership*, London: Saqi Books (2003), p. 258. This excellent volume contains a complete translation of Ibn Zafar's treatise, with notes and commentary. In *On Duties* II.7, Cicero notes that for a ruler "Fear is a poor sentry of long reliability; but devoted goodwill, on the other hand, can stand guard in perpetuity." See Curtius, Quintus, *On Duties*, Charleston: Fortress of the Mind Publications (2016), p. 120.

help, they could have forced open the doors and rescued him. The unarmed attackers were holding him alive while demanding a weapon from outside. When no one made any effort to save him, a Syracusan named Lyco handed through the windows a short sword with which Dion was killed.

10. Once the killing had taken place and a multitude arrived on the scene to find out what was happening, a few men were slain in the mistaken belief that they were involved in the assassination. For when the news quickly spread that violence had been used against Dion, many people who were disgusted by such outrages came running to the vicinity. These were the people who, inflamed by false suspicion, killed the innocent as if they were responsible parties. When word of his death was publicly announced, the public mood underwent a remarkable reversal. Those who had labeled him a tyrant when he was alive now called him a liberator of his country who had rescued it from a tyrant. Thus in an instant revulsion gave way to sympathy—so much so that Dion's people would have been willing to shed their own blood, if they could, to bring him back from Acheron.[174] He was given a public funeral and laid to rest in the busiest part of the city, with a prominent tomb marking the place of his interment. His death took place when he was about fifty-five years of age, in the fourth year after he had returned from the Peloponnesus to Sicily.

---

[174] A river in the Epirus district of Greece. It was believed to have a direct connection to the underworld.

XI. Iphicrates [C. 418 B.C.—C. 353 B.C.]

1. Iphicrates the Athenian was distinguished not so much by the importance of his deeds but by his unrivaled proficiency in military affairs. Not only was he a leader equal to the best commanders of his own era, but he should indeed be ranked ahead of the illustrious military men of earlier times as well. He lived and breathed war, often commanding armies, and never suffered a reversal that was traceable to his negligence. He always won by using his military acumen; and in this quality he was so impressive that he often produced innovations in military gear or refinements in what was already in use.[175] He was responsible for making significant changes to infantry weapons. Before he was a general it was customary to use large shields, short spears, and small swords; he, on the other hand, substituted crescent-shaped shields (*peltae*) for round shields (*parmae*).[176] Infantrymen have since been called peltasts as a consequence of this innovation; and he made this change so that soldiers would not have to carry so much weight when maneuvering or charging the enemy.

He doubled the length of the spear, and stretched the length of the sword. He ordered alterations to the infantryman's breastplate, replacing chain mail or bronze armor with a breastplate made of

---

[175] A sentence with nice cadence in the original: *Semper consilio vicit tantumque eo valuit, ut multa in re militari partim nova attulerit, partim meliora fecerit.*

[176] A *pelta* was a light, crescent-shaped shield. A *parma*, according to the Oxford Latin Dictionary, was a "small, usually round shield carried by light infantry and cavalry."

linen. These modifications resulted in an increase of his men's mobility. He lessened the weight they had to carry while being equally mindful of their need for protective equipment that fostered agility.

2. He went to war with the Thracians and brought Seuthes, an Athenian ally, back under his control.[177] He led his army at Corinth with such vigor that no forces were better trained or more responsive to command instruction.[178] He habituated his men with constant drill that, when the signal for battle was issued by the leader, they should align themselves in proper formation without requiring an order; each man appeared to be specifically placed there by a general of rare talent. He crushed an entire *mora*[179] of Lacedaemonians with this army, an achievement that was widely publicized all over Greece.[180] In another engagement during the same war he routed the entirety of their forces, a victory which won him wide acclaim.

When Artaxerxes decided to go to war against the king of Egypt, he asked the Athenians if he could hire Iphicrates to lead a mercenary army numbering twelve thousand men.[181] So rigorously trained was this force in all types of military drill that the expression "men of Iphicrates" became a badge of the highest praise among the Greeks, in the same way that at one time the "men of Fabius" were considered true Romans.[182] He once set out to render assistance to the Lacedaemonians and delayed the advance of Epaminondas;[183] and if his appearance had not been

---

[177] In 387 B.C.
[178] From 393 B.C. to 391 B.C.
[179] The *mora* was a division of the Spartan army. It contained between 500 and 900 men.
[180] This happened in 392 B.C.
[181] Iphicrates left for this assignment in 377 B.C.
[182] The Fabius referred to is Q. Fabius Maximus, the Roman opponent of Hannibal.
[183] In 369 B.C.

expected, the Thebans would not have hastily withdrawn from Sparta until they had occupied and burned the city.[184]

3. He had a greatness of soul as well as a general's bearing and stature, in a way that his countenance alone instilled veneration in whomever saw it. When it came to sustained exertion he had too little perseverance, as Theopompus has written; but he was a good citizen and a man of unimpeachable integrity. This quality showed itself on many occasions, but most notably in the instance when he protected the children of Amyntas the Macedonian. Eurydice, the mother of Perdiccas and Philippus,[185] fled with these two boys to Iphicrates, who made every effort to take care of her.[186] Girded by the affections of his fellow-citizens, he lived to an advanced age. He once had to answer to a capital charge; this was during the Social War,[187] at the same time Timotheus faced his own charge. Iphicrates was absolved of guilt.

He left behind a son named Mnestheus, born of a Thracian woman who was the daughter of King Cotus. When this son was asked whom he respected more, his father or his mother, his answer was: "My mother." When everyone was taken aback by this response, he continued: "I have good cause for saying this. As far as he could, my father reared me as a Thracian; but my mother, on the other hand, raised me to be an Athenian."

---

[184] Meaning that the Theban fear of Iphicrates was what made them rush to leave Sparta.
[185] Philip, father of Alexander the Great.
[186] These were the two surviving sons of Amyntas II of Macedonia. Eurydice fled to Iphicrates in 368 B.C. or 367 B.C. to protect her sons from Pausanias, the new claimant to the Macedonian throne.
[187] The Social War (from the Latin word *socii*, "allies") lasted from 357 B.C. to 355 B.C., and was waged between Athens and her dubious allies.

1546 woodcut depicting infantry combat, from Sebastian Münster's Cosmographia

XII. Chabrias [?—357 B.C.]

1. Chabrias, the Athenian. He is numbered among the very best military commanders and accomplished many great deeds that will be preserved in historical memory. But his feat that truly stands out was the stratagem he deployed in the battle he fought near Thebes, when he came to reinforce the Boeotians.[188] Here the great leader Agesilaus, once he had routed the mercenary units, felt confident of victory. Chabrias scuttled his plans; he forbade the rest of the army to cede its ground, and directed his men to brace themselves against the enemy attack with shields on knees and with each man's spear thrust forward. When Agesilaus saw this new technique, he dared not advance; and even though his men were already running to engage the other side, he recalled them using the battlefield trumpet. This gambit became so celebrated all over Greece that Chabrias wanted to be portrayed in this posture when his statue was publicly constructed at Athens's forum. A consequence of this was that athletes (and even artists) made a point of striking characteristic poses in the statues built to commemorate the victories they had achieved.

2. Chabrias, however, supervised many wars in Europe when he was an Athenian general. In Egypt he waged war on his own volition. When he set out to help Nectenebis, he consolidated his kingdom for him.[189] He carried out the same plan in Cyprus, but

---

[188] In 378 B.C.

[189] Chabrias was actually involved in Egypt two separate times, first in 377 B.C. and later in 361 B.C.

there he was tasked by the Athenians with helping Evagoras;[190] and he did not leave the island until he had entirely brought it under his control. The Athenians acquired significant glory as a result of this expedition. In the meantime the flame of war was ignited between the Egyptians and the Persians. The Athenians were allied with Artaxerxes, and the Lacedaemonians were aligned with the Egyptians—from whom the Lacedaemonian king Agesilaus was amassing great wealth. Chabrias realized this and, not wanting to cede any advantage to Agesilaus, set out on his own accord to help Egypt; he was put in charge of the Egyptian fleet, while Agesilaus had control over the infantry units.

3. The Persian king's prefects then sent emissaries to Athens to voice their displeasure that Chabrias, with the help of the Egyptians, was waging war against their king. The Athenians set a specific deadline for Chabiras to return home, and made it clear that he would face the death penalty if he did not comply. In response to this message he returned to Athens, but remained there no longer than was necessary. He had no desire to subject himself to the scrutinizing gazes of his fellow citizens; for he was living sumptuously and luxuriating himself too wantonly to be able to avoid the disapproval of the masses. In fact, a common defect in great and free republics is that glory's junior partner is jealousy. People love tearing down those whom they see gaining more prominence than others; and the rabble cannot maintain a neutral attitude while observing the good fortune of others who are wealthy. Chabrias, therefore, stayed away as much as he could.

Neither was he the only one who consciously kept away from Athens: most of the important men did the same thing. They believed that the more they withdrew from public view, the more they would be able to avoid the envy of others. Thus Conon frequently made his home in Cyprus, Iphicrates in Thrace, Timotheus

---

[190] Evagoras (or Euagoras) I (411 B.C.—374 B.C.), the king of Salamis in Cyprus.

in Lesbos, and Chares at Sigeum. With regard to deeds and personal attributes, Chares was not like the previously mentioned names; but he was an honored figure in Athens and had considerable influence there.

4. However, Chabrias died during the Social War in this way. The Athenians were assaulting Chios.[191] Chabrias had an unofficial position,[192] but exceeded the authority of all others who held official ranks, and the soldiers looked to him for guidance rather than to their supervisory officers. This was what accelerated his death. He wanted to be the first man to reach the port, and so ordered his helmsman to guide the ship there—and in this way he sealed his own doom. When he entered the port, the other ships did not follow him. He was thus encircled by the enemy; and although he resisted ferociously, his ship foundered after having been struck by a ram.[193] He might have saved himself by leaping into the sea—since the nearby Athenian fleet could pull swimmers out of the water—but he chose to go down with his ship rather than throw away his weapons and relinquish the vessel he had commanded. The rest of his crew chose not to follow his example, and swam to safety. But Chabrias, believing that an honorable death was better than a disgraceful life, was killed by enemy weapons while fighting at close quarters.

---

[191] An Aegean island off the coast of Ionia.
[192] The phrase used is *classe privatus*, meaning "personal grade" or "private levy."
[193] Literally, "struck by a beak" (*rostro percussa*). Ancient warships were often equipped with a ram in the form of a metal-tipped bird's beak.

An image of a coastal town, from Sebastian Münster's Cosmographia *(1546)*

XIII. Timotheus [?—354 B.C.]

1. Timotheus, the Athenian, son of Conon. He augmented the prestige conferred on him by his father with many brave achievements of his own. He was articulate, dynamic, and hard-working. Adroit in military affairs, he was no less capable in the art of civil administration. His superlative deeds are many in number, but these are his most famous. He subjugated with force the Olynthians and Byzantines.[194] He captured Samos; and although the Athenians in a previous conflict[195] had expended twelve hundred talents trying to take the island, Timotheus returned Samos to the Athenian people without any cost to the state.[196] He went to war against Cotus and won twelve hundred talents' worth of spoils which he gave to the state.[197]

He liberated Cyzicus[198] from a siege. He set out with Agesilaus to help Ariobarzanes;[199] and while the Laconian took a monetary payment from Ariobarzanes, Timotheus wanted his fellow citizens to add to their lands and cities, rather than himself accept riches of which he could bring home only a portion. Thus he accepted Crithote and Sestus.[200]

---

[194] In 364 B.C.
[195] In 440 B.C.
[196] I.e., the spoils of the war paid for its costs.
[197] Around 363 B.C.
[198] A city in the Propontis in Asia Minor.
[199] Persian satrap of Phrygia.
[200] Towns in Thrace.

2. When he was put in charge of the fleet, he sailed around the Peloponnesus and plundered the Laconians;[201] he routed their fleet and forced Corcyra to submit to Athenian rule. To the Athenian alliance system he also added the Epirotes, Athamanes, Chaones, and all those peoples living near that region of the sea. Once this happened, the Lacedaemonians concluded a drawn-out struggle, and on their own accord ceded hegemony in naval power to the Athenians; they consented to peace terms that granted Athens undisputed control of the seas. This victory brought such euphoria to the people of Attica that for the first time they publicly dedicated an altar to the goddess of Peace, and created a *pulvinar*[202] for this goddess as well. To preserve the memory of his achievement, the people erected a statue to Timotheus in the Athenian forum at public expense. This was an honor which came to him alone up to that time; that is, when the people set up a statue to a father, they set up one for the son as well.[203] Thus the more recent statue of the son, placed beside the statue of his father, renewed the public's fading recollection of the father.

3. When he had reached old age and no longer held a political position, the Athenians faced the prospect of armed conflict everywhere they looked: Samos was rebellious, the Hellespont had defected, and Philip—who was even then a force to be reckoned with—was conducting his own schemes in Macedon. Chares was the man assigned to stop Philip, but he was not thought to be strong enough for the task. Menestheus, the son of Iphicrates and son-in-law of Timotheus, was then appointed commander, and it

---

[201] In 375 B.C.
[202] A *pulvinar*, according to the Oxford Latin Dictionary, is a "cushioned couch, one of several on which images of gods were placed at a *lectisternium*. The word was also used "singly in commemoration of particular gods." Its purpose was to provide a physical image before which people could leave ritual offerings.
[203] Nepos apparently means that "no one else had this honor before that time," but his wording could have been clearer.

was determined that he should go off to war. He was given two men—his father and his son-in-law—to serve as advisors; they were highly respected for their experience and professional judgment. Their prestige was great enough to generate hope that, with their participation, what had previously been lost might now be regained.

They then set out for Samos. Chares, who knew they were on their way, hastened to get there as well, out of fear that it might look like decisions were being made without him. When they were approaching the island, a huge storm blew in; the two veteran commanders, knowing it would be advantageous to give it a wide berth, halted the fleet. But Chares was rash: acting as if he could direct Fortune with his own hands, he refused to listen to the consummate judgment of his seniors. He arrived at the place he had intended, and sent word to Timotheus and Iphicrates that they could follow him there.

Then disaster struck. After losing a number of ships, he limped back to his starting point; he then sent an official account to Athens claiming he could easily have taken Samos had he not been abandoned by Timotheus and Iphicrates. The Athenian people were volatile, suspicious, and consequently fickle; they were also prickly and jealous, and in this case the accused happened to be men of influence. They were all recalled to Athens and forced to respond to charges of treason. Timotheus was convicted and fined the sum of one hundred talents. Seething with resentment over his country's lack of gratitude, he moved to Chalcis.[204]

4. After his death, the people regretted this verdict against him and abated nine-tenths of the fine; Athens ordered his son Conon to pay ten talents for the rebuilding of part of the city walls. The variability of Fortune is clearly on display in this episode. For the grandson Conon was forced to restore, from his own funds and with great humiliation to his family, the same walls that his grandfather, using plunder taken from enemies, had reconstructed for his country. Timotheus's life was characterized by wisdom and

---

[204] A town in Euboea

moderation; and although I could relate many anecdotes to confirm this, I shall be satisfied to offer one, from which one may readily conclude how beloved he was to his friends.

When he was a youth at Athens and became embroiled in legal action,[205] not only did his friends in Athens and in other states come to his defense, but even Jason, the tyrant of Thessaly, was counted among these—and at that time Jason was the most powerful of all. This ruler, even though he did not consider himself safe even in his own country without attendants, came to Athens without a single bodyguard. He thought so highly of his honored comrade[206] that he preferred to incur life-threatening risk than to abandon Timotheus when he was fighting to preserve his good name. Nevertheless, Timotheus later made war against Jason at the behest of Athenian public sentiment; he believed his country's legal rights were more inviolate than the covenant of hospitality.

With Iphicrates, Chabrias, and Timotheus, we reach the end of the era of the Athenian generals; after their deaths we find no commander in that city who is worthy of recollection. I now come to the most courageous and brilliant of all the barbarians—excepting the two Carthaginians, Hamilcar and Hannibal. Since his accomplishments are less well-known, and because he achieved his victories not through the size of his forces but as a result of his superior judgment, an attribute in which he surpassed all his peers, I will provide more information about his career. Unless the causes of his victories are described, his merits as a commander cannot be grasped.

---

[205] In 373 B.C.

[206] The word used is *hospes*, a term that has no precise English equivalent. The Oxford Latin Dictionary defines it as "a person bound to one of another town, country, etc., by personal or inherited ties of hospitality." It was a covenanted relationship of a type that is not found in modern industrial societies; and it carried certain duties, such as an obligation to provide sanctuary to the other.

Two opposing forces collide. A woodcut from the Cosmographia *(1546)*

XIV. Datames [?—362 B.C.]

1. Datames was a Carian by birth. His mother was Scythian, and his father was Camisares. He originally was one of the soldiers assigned to security duty at the palace of Artaxerxes. His father Camisares was known for his fearlessness and proficiency in war, and had repeatedly demonstrated his loyalty to the king; he managed that part of the province of Cilicia adjacent to Cappadocia which is inhabited by the Leucosyri.[207] During his term of service as a soldier, Datames's skills first became apparent during the war the king prosecuted against the Cadusii.[208] In this conflict—despite the fact that many thousands of the king's men had been killed—his contributions were of crucial importance. A result was that, since Camisares had been killed during the war, Datames inherited the command of his father's province.

2. Afterwards he demonstrated he was just as exemplary in martial virtue when Autophrodates[209] went to war, on the king's orders, against those who had committed sedition. For when enemy forces had penetrated the king's camp, it was due to Datames's efforts that they were put to flight and the rest of the king's army was kept intact. An outcome of this success was that he came to be assigned more important responsibilities. There was at that time a man named Thuys, a ruler of Paphlagonia;[210] he was

---

[207] A Greek term literally meaning "White Syrians." The Leucosyri were an Anatolian tribe of apparently mixed Iranian, Hittite, and Syrian origin.
[208] A tribe located in Media. The war took place from 358 B.C. to 380 B.C.
[209] The satrap of Lydia.
[210] A region in northern Anatolia adjacent to the Black Sea.

from an ancient family and could trace his lineage to that Pylaemenes[211] who (as Homer says) was killed by Patroclus during the Trojan War. He was ignoring the royal decrees, so the king decided to undertake a punitive expedition against him. Datames, a close relative of the Paphlagonian, was appointed to lead the campaign. It happened that Datames and Thuys had parents who were brother and sister, respectively.[212] For this reason Datames first wanted to try to persuade his relative to fulfill his responsibilities without resorting to armed action. He went to visit Thuys without a detachment of soldiers, as he was not suspecting perfidious behavior from a friend. But for Datames this step nearly proved to be fatal, because his kinsman tried to assassinate him covertly.

Datames's mother was with him, and she was the paternal aunt[213] of the Paphlagonian. She learned of the scheme that was being planned and warned her son in advance. Datames escaped the trap and declared war on Thuys. Although during the war he lost the support of Ariobarzanes, prefect of Lydia, Ionia, and all of Phrygia, he persevered with unrelenting intensity and captured Thuys alive, along with his wife and children.

3. Datames made a dedicated effort to ensure that the king did not get wind of these events before he himself arrived. He came to where the king was without anyone discovering his identity. The next day he ordered Thuys to be dressed; he was a man of imposing size and intimidating appearance because of his dark complexion, long hair, and unkempt beard. Datames outfitted him in the lush garments that the king's satraps commonly wear, and garnished him with a necklace of twisted metal,[214] gold bracelets, and other princely accessories. Datames himself put on a commoner's doubled cloak and woolen tunic, and on his head wore a hunter's hat; he carried a club in his right hand and a rope in his

---

[211] A mythical early king of the Paphlagonians.
[212] Meaning that Datames's father and the Paphlagonian's mother were brother and sister.
[213] *Amita* (paternal aunt) is the word used.
[214] *Torquis*: a tight necklace of braided or twisted metal.

left, the end of which was tied to Thuys. Datames walked the fettered Thuys before him in this fashion as if he were handling a newly-captured wild animal.[215]

Thuys's bizarre clothing and strange aspect soon drew everyone's attention. A large crowd soon collected; someone inevitably recognized Thuys and passed this information to the king. Artaxerxes at first did not believe the story and sent Pharnabazus to gather additional details. The king was told what had happened, and ordered them both to be brought before him; he was delighted with the seizure of Thuys and with the way Datames had dressed him up. Artaxerxes was especially grateful that the renegade king had unexpectedly been delivered into his hands. He thus rewarded Datames handsomely and assigned him to the army, which was then being readied by Pharnabazus and Tithraustes for military operations in Egypt; and with these two men the king delegated him equal command responsibility. Indeed when the king later removed Pharnabazus, supreme command was turned over to Datames.

4. While he was intensely focused on outfitting the army and arranging its embarkation to Egypt, the king abruptly sent him a letter with instructions to attack Aspis, the ruler of Cataonia. This nation is situated beyond Cilicia and has a common boundary with Cappadocia. Aspis, living in a region of wooded valleys and well-defended fortresses, not only refused to recognize the Persian king's suzerainty, but he conducted raids against nearby regions to steal goods intended for the king.

Although Datames was far away from these places and was preoccupied with more important assignments, he nevertheless believed it was his responsibility to obey the king's directive. He therefore boarded a ship, along with a few (but brave) men, believing that it would be easier to destroy an unsuspecting enemy with a small force than a prepared enemy with a vastly larger force.[216] And this is exactly what happened.

---

[215] The goal of this charade was to humiliate Thuys and to entertain the king.

[216] Meaning that surprise was what mattered: *facilius se imprudentem parva manu oppressurum quam paratum quamvis magno exercitu.*

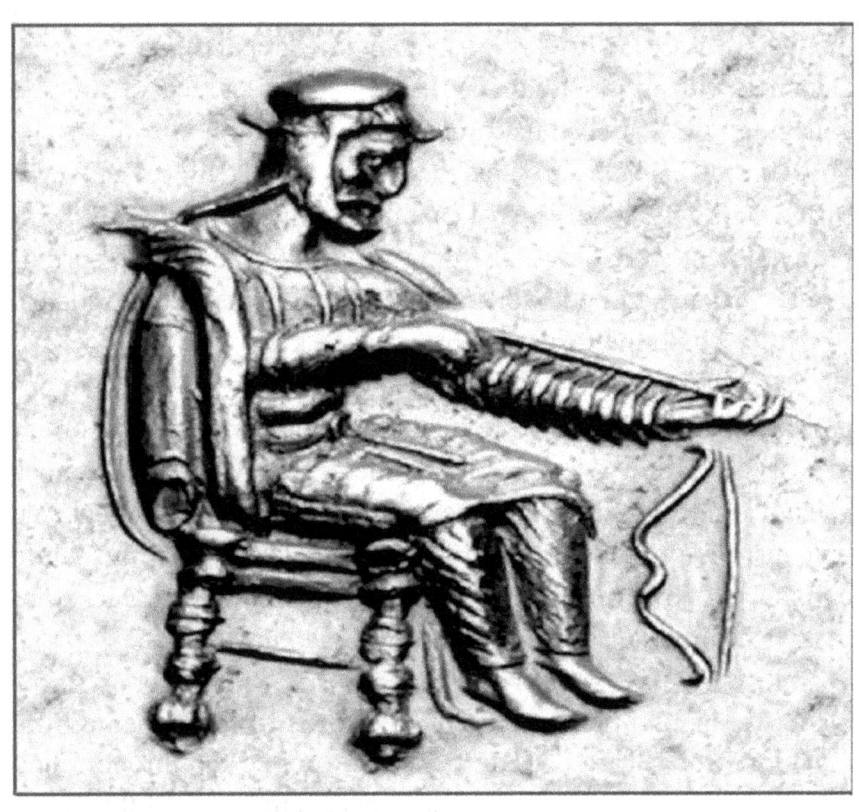

Datames inspecting an arrow in Persian dress. Beautiful detail from a Cilician coin struck about 375 B.C. His name in Aramaic, "Tarkumuwa," also appears on this coin (not visible here). Image courtesy of Classical Numismatic Group, LLC (www.cngcoins.com).

Having made the voyage to Cilicia and landing there, he traveled overland for a day and a night, crossed the Taurus, and came to the location he had intended. Datames asked the locals where Aspis was and learned that he was close by, having just left to go hunting. While he was conducting a reconnaissance of the area, the purpose of his incursion leaked out. In addition to using the men who were with him, Aspis made preparations to resist Datames with the Pisidians. When Datames learned of this, he collected his weapons, and ordered his men to go after them; he himself rode his horse towards the enemy at full gallop. Aspis was seized with fear as he spied Datames coming towards him from far away; and, deciding not to put up a fight, he simply surrendered. Datames turned over the shackled prisoner to Mithridates, so that he could then be transported to the king.

5. As these events were taking place, Artaxerxes began to appreciate that he had diverted his best general from an important military operation to a minor assignment. Believing that Datames had not yet departed, the king sent a messenger to the army at Ace with instructions that the general should not leave the army. While on his way, however, the messenger encountered the detachment that was delivering Aspis in custody to the king.

Although Datames earned a great deal of royal goodwill for his fast response, he also became the focus of more than a little malicious envy from the courtiers who orbited the throne. They knew that this one man was more respected than any of them. For this reason they agreed among themselves that he must be removed from the picture. Pandantes, the guardian of the king's treasure and a friend of Datames, sent him a letter disclosing the conspiracy; he made it clear that Datames would be in great danger should he experience any military setback during his command in Egypt. For it was in the nature of kings to blame failures on the men who served them, while attributing favorable endeavors to their own good fortune. It followed from this that they were easily persuaded to destroy those generals who allegedly suffered military reversals; and Datames would be at greater risk because he had aroused the implacable hostility of those at court who most had the king's ear.

Datames read the letter by the time he reached the army at Ace; and because he knew its contents were true, he decided to resign his command. Yet never did he take any action that would reflect dishonorably on him. He set up Mandrocles of Magnesia as leader of the army; and Datames himself—never revealing his true feelings about the king—left for Cappadocia with some of his own men and settled in the adjoining region of Paphlagonia. He then formed a secret friendship with Ariobarzanes, put together a group of soldiers, and gave the fortified cities the responsibility to protect his friends.

6. Because of the intervention of winter, these initial steps did show much in the way of progress. Datames heard that the Pisidians were preparing a force to move against him; he dispatched his son Arsidaeus with an army to confront this threat; and the youth was killed in the ensuing battle. The father, hiding the severity of the wound he had received, then set out to find them, accompanied by a force that was not too numerous. His goal was to find the enemy before word of the disaster reached his men, lest the news of his son's death have a debilitating effect on the soldiers' morale. He reached his objective, and so positioned his camp that he could neither be encircled by the enemy's substantial numbers nor be hindered in preparing his men for an engagement.

Datames had with him his father-in-law Mithrobarzanes as cavalry leader. Believing the situation was hopeless, however, he defected to the other side. When Datames learned of this, he realized that if word circulated among the men that he had been abandoned by such a close relative, everyone else would want to do the same thing. He therefore let it be known that Mithrobarzanes was acting under orders[217] when he had gone over to the other side as a deserter, so that he could more easily kill the enemy

---

[217] This same ruse was used by Hannibal when he first entered Italy. Some units deserted him, and to prevent the defeatist virus from spreading, he acted as if he had dismissed them voluntarily.

once he had been taken into their confidence. For this reason, he said, it would not be right to leave him; they should instead follow him immediately. If they took action imbued with unshakable will, the enemy would be unable to offer any resistance, as they would be facing slaughter from both inside and outside their ramparts.

Once this plan was accepted, he led out his army and set off after Mithrobarzanes; and when the latter reached the enemy lines, Datames issued the order to attack. The Pisidians were thrown off balance by this bizarre situation, and began to think the deserters were acting in bad faith. They concluded that this was a stratagem whereby the deserters, once received, would then turn on them, resulting in an even greater calamity. Datames's men first went after the deserters. The traitors could not comprehend what was happening, nor did they know why they were being attacked: they were forced to fight those to whom they had tried to desert, and stand alongside those whom they had abandoned.

Neither side spared them, and they were quickly slaughtered. Datames then struck at the remaining Pisidians who offered resistance. He drove them away with the first assault, pursued those who fled, killed a great number of them, and captured the enemy camp. Using this tactic Datames at the same time both annihilated the traitors in his own ranks and crushed his enemy. A scheme that had been designed to produce his downfall, he instead converted into the instrument of his deliverance. Nowhere else have I read of a more cunning maneuver by any general, nor of any battlefield gambit implemented with such speed.

7. Nevertheless Datames was betrayed by his eldest son Sysinas, who went to see the king and conveyed the news of his father's desertion. Artaxerxes was much troubled upon hearing this, since he realized he would now have to match wits with a resourceful and vigorous opponent who was ready to act decisively when he set his mind to something, and who always deliberated before making any moves. The king sent Autophrodates to

Cappadocia.[218] To bar his entrance, Datames wanted to seize the mountain pass where the Cilician Gates[219] were located; but he was unable to march his forces there quickly enough. After this setback, he and his men picked a location that both protected them from encirclement by the enemy, and also allowed them to attack from two sides any adversary trying to move past their position. If the enemy wanted to fight in that spot, their superior numbers would not be so decisive against Datames's smaller force.

8. Autophrodates understood the disposition of forces, but chose to meet his opponent in battle instead of withdrawing so large a force or encamping in one location for an extended period. He had with him twenty thousand barbarian cavalry and a hundred thousand infantry. Of the soldiers that the Persians call Cardaces,[220] there were three thousand slingers of this origin; there were also eight thousand Cappadocians, ten thousand Armenians, five thousand Paphlagonians, ten thousand Phrygians, five thousand Lydians, around three thousand Aspendians[221] and Pisidians, two thousand Cilicians with an equal number of Captiani, and three thousand Greek mercenaries. There was also a great number of lightly-armed foot soldiers.

Since he did not even have one-twentieth of the number of men fielded by his enemy, Datames's only hope in making a stand against such a force was to rely on the favorability of his position. He trusted to the resources he had, met the enemy in combat, and killed thousands of them; the fatalities in his own army numbered not more than a thousand. The day after the battle he constructed a monument at the location where he had fought the previous day, and then broke camp and left. In every battle he always overcame superior numbers with a smaller force, because he never committed his army unless he had confined his adversary in some narrow

---

[218] To deal with Datames.
[219] A mountain pass leading from Cilicia to Cappadocia.
[220] The name given to a class of mercenary Persian soldiers.
[221] Aspendus was a city in Pamphylia.

terrain feature: his knowledge of the region and thorough planning meant that this often occurred. When Autophrodates realized that protracted fighting was becoming more ruinous for the king than for the king's enemies, he floated the idea of peace and friendship as a way to repair relations with the throne. Although he had little trust in this offer, Datames agreed to the proposal and said he would send representatives to Artaxerxes. Thus was concluded the war that the Persian king had launched against him. Autophrodates brought his forces back to Phrygia.

9. Yet the king by now nursed an unrelenting hatred of Datames; he was aware that he could not beat him on the battlefield, and so conceived the idea of killing him with treachery. Yet the general avoided many of the king's snares. Thus when he was told that some men whom he believed were friends were in fact plotting against him, he took the position that such accusations made by a man's personal enemies should be neither believed nor ignored. Datames wanted to verify for himself whether what he had been told was true or false.

So he went to find the location on the road where the ambush against him was supposed to happen. But Datames picked a substitute who was similar to him in size and build, dressed him in his own clothing, and told him to march in that position where he himself would normally be.[222] The general, outfitted and dressed as a regular soldier, then placed himself among his bodyguards and began the march forward. When the column reached the ambush location, the assassins,[223] tricked by the decoy's appearance and position in the line, launched their attack against Datames's substitute. But the general had already warned his marching comrades to be prepared to act when they saw him take action. And when he noticed the ambushers running towards the line, Datames

---

[222] I.e., that the "body double" should take Datames's normal spot in the group's column (*agmen*).
[223] *Insidiatores*, or those who lie in wait to attack.

flung spears at them; everyone else followed his example, and the would-be killers were soon cut to pieces, their bodies thoroughly rent with projectiles.

10. As shrewd as he was, however, this man was ultimately ensnared by the guile of Mithridates, the son of Ariobarzanes. For he had made assurances to the king that he would kill Datames as long as the king gave him complete freedom of action without any restraints, and would give him his word of honor—according to Persian custom—with a raised right hand. When he received this guarantee from a messenger sent by the king, Mithridates gathered his forces and, although far away from Datames, made overtures of friendship with him. He then started harassing the king's territories, raiding his fortresses, and carrying off a good deal of plunder; he divided some of these spoils among his own men, and sent some to Datames. In similar fashion he gave Datames several captured fortresses.

By continuing this pattern of activity for some time, Mithridates persuaded him that he had launched an all-out war against the king. Yet in order not to arouse any suspicion of trickery, Mithridates neither sought a conference with his target nor tried to meet him in person. Thus, although he was far away from Datames, he wore the mask of friendship in such a way that the two of them appeared to be linked—not by joint operations, but by the mutual hostility they had for the king.

11. Once Mithridates thought he had adequately communicated his intentions, he let Datames know that the time had come to prepare larger military forces and commence direct operations against the king. He asked Datames to meet him for discussions, if this was acceptable, at any location he preferred. The general agreed to the proposition, a conference time was agreed on, and a location was selected. Mithridates traveled to the agreed place several days beforehand with one of his most trusted attendants, and buried swords in several spots which he diligently noted. On the day of the conference both sides sent people to look over the

location and to search the two leaders personally; after this, the two of them finally began discussions.

After an extended dialogue with each other, they each went away in different directions. Once Datames was a good distance away, Mithridates—in order not to create any suspicion—returned to the conference spot before going back to the rest of his men. He sat down at a place where a weapon was buried, as if he needed to recover from fatigue; he then called out to Datames to return to the conference spot, on the pretext that some issue had been omitted from their earlier discussion. During this time he brought out the buried sword, removed it from its scabbard, and hid it in his clothing. When Datames arrived at the meeting place, Mithridates said that as he was leaving he had observed a certain spot—visible from where they were now—that was appropriate for setting up a camp. He extended a finger to point out the location, and Datames turned his body to look; Mithridates then thrust the sword into his back, killing him before anyone could render assistance. Thus was this remarkable man, who had overcome so many others with superior planning but none with duplicity, ultimately led to ruin by false friendship.

Frontispiece of a 1667 edition of Nepos

XV. Epaminondas [?—362 B.C.][224]

1. Epaminondas the Theban, the son of Polymnis. Before I begin my biography of this commander, readers should be cautioned not to form judgments on the customs of other peoples by comparing them to their own ways. Neither should they believe that what is scandalous to themselves is viewed the same way by others. Indeed, in our own culture, we know that music is not an appropriate pastime for a person of distinction; to be sure, even dancing is considered a vice. For the Greeks, however, all of these activities were seen as acceptable and worthy of praise.

Since I want to paint a picture of Epaminondas's life and personal habits, it is clear that I should not leave out anything that is relevant to this objective. Accordingly we will first discuss his family background, then the disciplines he studied and who tutored him; we will also consider his character, personal qualities, and whatever else that may be worth mentioning. Lastly we will explain his great deeds, which many people value more highly than the virtues of the mind.

2. He was born of the father I identified above, and came from respectable family, although not one that had inherited significant wealth. No other Theban, however, received an education better than his. He was taught by Dionysius to play the lyre and to sing together with musical instruments; this teacher was no less famous in the field of music than Damon or Lamprus, whose names

---

[224] This biography of Epaminondas is one of the principal ancient sources of information on his life. Plutarch's account of his life has not survived.

have achieved great renown. From Olympiodorus he learned how to play the flute, and from Calliphron how to dance. His tutor in philosophy was Lysis of Tarentum, the Pythagorean; he was so dedicated to this instructor that as a youth he valued his relationship with this dour and ascetic old man more than any of his friendships with his peers. He did not discharge his teacher until he had surpassed in learning all his other schoolmates. It could clearly be observed from this fact that he would likewise outdistance everyone in other fields of endeavor. Now these activities are seen by us as unimportant, even frivolous; but in Greece they were highly regarded disciplines, especially in Epaminondas's day.

After he reached puberty and began to train at the palaestra,[225] he did not blindly chase after the acquisition of brute physical strength, but instead made speed of movement his goal. For the former quality he believed would be useful in the arena of sports, while the latter would be important in war. To this end, Epaminondas focused his training efforts on running and wrestling—but only enough wrestling to enable him to clinch and grapple with an adversary while standing. In fact the majority of his training time was spent on gaining proficiency with weapons.

---

[225] Wrestling school or gymnasium.

A sixteenth century woodcut portrait of Epaminondas

3. Even more impressive mental qualities were added to his robustness of body. He was modest, prudent, serious, shrewd in the use of available opportunities, expert in war, physically strong, possessed of an expansive spirit,[226] and so scrupulous in observing the truth that he never even lied as a joke. He was also restrained, tolerant, and patient to a surprising degree: he could endure injuries not only from the people, but even from his close friends. He paid scrupulous attention to concealing the essentials of his plans, a habit that is sometimes just as advantageous as speaking eloquently; and he was adept at listening to others, for he believed that this was the quickest way to gain information about his environment. Thus whenever he was at some meeting where politics was discussed, or where philosophy was being debated, he never left until the conversation was concluded.

He so easily tolerated his lack of wealth that he gained nothing from his service to the state except glory. He refrained from using his friends' resources for his own benefit; and he so enjoyed the trust of others when he helped them that it is tempting to think he and his friends owned everything communally. If any of his fellow Thebans were ever captured by the enemy,[227] or if a young girl eligible for marriage could not secure a husband due to her inability to provide a dowry, he discussed the matter with his friends and ordered the amount each man would donate according to his resources. When he put together the required sum (and before he actually accepted the money), he brought the debtor in front of those who had donated the funds, so that the debtor would know how much he owed each person.

4. His honesty was put to the test by Diomedon of Cyzicus. At the behest of King Artaxerxes,[228] Diomedon tried to corrupt Epaminondas with offers of money. He showed up at Thebes with

---

[226] Nepos uses the phrase *animo maximo* here, which could also refer to his expansive intellect or character.
[227] And needed to be ransomed.
[228] Artaxerxes Mnemon. This incident took place around 374 B.C.

a large amount of gold and, for the price of five talents, bought the compliance of a young man named Micythus whom Epaminondas very much cared for. Micythus met with Epaminondas and disclosed to him the reason why Diomedon had come to Thebes.

But Epaminondas made a personal visit to Diomedon and told him, "There is no need to resort to money. For if what the king wants is in the interests of the Theban people, I am ready to do it for free. If, however, the opposite is true, then no amount of gold he may offer will persuade me to accept it. I would not accept the riches of the entire world as a substitute for the love of my country. I am not surprised you have tried to bribe me, without knowing what kind of man I am, believing me to be just like you. For this I forgive you. But so that you do not corrupt others, you must go now without delay, since you were unable to have your way with me. And you, Micythus, return this man's money to him. I will turn you in to the magistrates unless you do it at once."

When Diomedon asked if he could safely leave and take the money he had carried to Thebes, Epaminondas said, "I will allow you to do this. Not for your sake, but for mine. If you were deprived of your money, I worry someone might say that what I refused to accept as a bribe came instead to me through legal forfeiture." He then asked the foreigner where he wanted to be escorted, and the Persian told him he wanted to go to Athens. Epaminondas even gave him a security detail to make sure he arrived safely. Even this was insufficient for him; with the help of Chabrias the Athenian—whom we mentioned earlier—he made sure the Persian was not harmed before he boarded his ship to leave.

This will be sufficient confirmation of his integrity. Actually I could offer a great many other anecdotes, but I must adhere to my original purpose. It has been my goal to relate the lives of a number of exceptional men in this one volume, and many prominent writers before me have already composed thousands of lines about them.

5. He was also so eloquent that no other Theban could rival him in expressive power. Nor was he any less artful in his short responses than he was elegant in his extended orations. Epaminondas had one particularly harsh Theban critic named Meneclides, someone who was an adversary in government service. At least by Theban standards, he was well-trained in public speaking; for the people of this region are more noted for physical strength than for intellectual accomplishment. Because Meneclides saw that Epaminondas blossomed during times of military action, he was in the habit of pleading with the Thebans to seek peaceful solutions instead of war, so that they would not be in need of the skills of that brilliant commander. Epaminondas told him, "When you divert the attention of your fellow citizens away from war by speaking this way, you are being dishonest with them. You are actually advocating for slavery dressed up in the costume of peace: for peace is acquired through war. Those who wish to bask in peace's rays for some time should be thoroughly trained in warfare. So if you want to be Greece's preeminent city, you should be spending your time in camp instead of the gymnasium."

When this same Meneclides scolded him for not marrying or having children—and particularly for having the insolence to suppose he had rivaled Agamemnon's[229] prestige in war—Epaminondas gave the following response. "Meneclides, stop berating me for not having a wife. For when it comes to this issue, there is no man's advice I want to follow less than yours." (Meneclides had, as a matter of fact, come under suspicion for marital infidelity). "And if," he continued, "you think I am comparing myself with Agamemnon as an equal, you are deluding yourself. For he needed just about ten years to take one city,[230]

---

[229] The commander of the Greek forces during the Trojan War.
[230] I.e., Troy.

despite having all of Greece to help him. On the other hand, I myself with this one city of ours defeated the Lacedaemonians in a single day[231] and liberated the whole of Greece."

6. When Epaminondas approached the convention of the Arcadians to ask them to form a mutual assistance treaty with the Thebans and Argives, the Athenian envoy Callistratus (who surpassed everyone else in eloquence at that time) argued against this suggestion. He proposed that it would be better to conclude a treaty of friendship with the people of Attica. In his speech he railed angrily against the Argives and Thebans; he asserted that the Arcadians should evaluate the quality of some people coming from these two cities, as a sample from which they might judge the rest of them. So Orestes and Alcmaeon, who had murdered their mothers, came from Argos; and so Oedipus the Theban produced children with his mother after slaying his father.[232]

Once he had disposed of some ancillary topics, Epaminondas decided to respond to Callistratus's insults. He said he was astonished by the Attic orator's stupidity in failing to comprehend that the men he had mentioned were innocent in their homelands at the time of their births. Once they committed their crimes, they were promptly expelled from their native lands—*and were then taken in by the Athenians.*[233]

Yet the most impressive example of his eloquence took place at Sparta where he was serving as an envoy before the Battle of Leuctra. All the envoys of the allied cities had convened there. Speaking personally to that huge assembly of representatives, he

---

[231] Referring to the Battle of Leuctra in 371 B.C.
[232] Orestes, the son of Agamemnon, killed his mother Clytaemnestra after she had killed Orestes's father. Alcmaeon of Argos slew his mother Eriphyle in revenge for convincing Alcmaeon's father Amphiaraus to participate in a doomed expedition. These were apparently mythical figures, but many Greeks believed the legends had a factual basis.
[233] As Callistratus was the legate of the Athenians, Epaminondas turned the insult back on him with this response.

so stridently attacked the Lacedaemonian tyranny that his oration succeeded in eroding Spartan power no less profoundly than did the Battle of Leuctra. For as later events would show, this speech was what isolated the Lacedaemonians from any support by their allies.

7. The following anecdotes demonstrate his conviction that, because it was a violation of divine law to become embittered towards one's nation, a man must be forbearing and willing to suffer ill-treatment from one's fellow-citizens. Because of jealousy directed towards Epaminondas, the Thebans did not want to appoint him to lead their army, selecting instead a man without command experience. When this general's error of judgment caused the multitude of soldiers to fear for their safety—because they were trapped in a narrow pass and besieged by the enemy—the necessity of having Epaminondas's special ability became clear. He happened to be there, in fact, serving as a private soldier.[234]

When they sought his counsel on what to do, he did not nurse any resentment over the shabby treatment he had received. He freed the army from its blockade and led it home without loss of life. Neither did he do this just once: he did it very often. A truly brilliant example of this was the time he led the army to the Peloponnesus against the Lacedaemonians and had two colleagues, one of whom was Pelopidas, a man of prodigious strength and vigor.

Because of the accusations leveled against them by their political enemies, all these generals eventually had a considerable amount of malice directed at them; in the end they were stripped of their commands and succeeded by others chosen to replace them. Epaminondas did not yield to the people's decision; he convinced his colleagues to do the same, and resumed the war that he had initiated. He knew that unless he took this course of action, the entire army would be lost, owing to the ineptitude of the other commanders and their conspicuous lack of battlefield experience.

---

[234] This took place in 368 B.C., during an expedition to Thessaly.

A compelling 1814 depiction of Epaminondas at a conference

Now there was a Theban statute that mandated the death penalty for anyone who retained his command beyond the expiration date decreed by law. Since Epaminondas knew that this statute had been enacted to preserve the Theban republic, he did not want it to bring calamity to the country. So he held on to his command for four months beyond the date set by the people for its expiration.

8. When he returned home, his colleagues were indicted for violating the law just mentioned. He permitted his subordinates to pin the blame on him for what had happened, and he allowed them to assert that the decision to break the law had been entirely his doing. This defense removed them from harm's way. No one believed that Epaminondas would respond to the statements, since he could have nothing of importance to say. Yet he appeared before the tribunal and denied none of the accusations made by his adversaries; he conceded everything his colleagues had stated, and willingly submitted to the punishment mandated by law.

He requested only one thing from the tribunal, and this was that they should make the following official entry as part of the trial record: "Epaminondas was sentenced to death by the Thebans because he forced them to defeat the Lacedaemonians at Leuctra. Before he became general no Theban had dared to face the Lacedaemonians on the battlefield. In one battle he not only rescued Thebes from ruin, but also won freedom for the whole of Greece. He so decisively shaped events for each side that it was the Thebans who attacked the Spartans, while the Spartans were happy just being able to save themselves. And, once Messene[235] had been restored to independence, he did not conclude the war until he laid siege to Sparta." When he said this, everyone present was convulsed with hearty laughter, and not a single juror dared to vote in favor of the prescribed punishment. In this way did he emerge with the greatest glory after facing a capital charge.

---

[235] A town located in the southwestern part of the Peloponnesus. It had been under Spartan control for some time, and Epaminondas wished to restore its independence.

9. Ultimately, however, when he was the commanding general at Mantinea[236] and the battle-line had been prepared, he pressed too recklessly against the enemy, and the Lacedaemonians were able to identify him. Since they knew the removal of this one man would guarantee their country's security, they all went after Epaminondas and did not stop—amid great slaughter and the deaths of many men—until they saw him collapse while fighting, hit by a javelin[237] thrown from a distance. The Boeotians were delayed for some time as a result of his death, but they did not disengage until they had thoroughly routed their adversaries. But when Epaminondas realized he had sustained a mortal wound, and also saw that he would immediately perish[238] if he removed the spearhead that had detached from its shaft and remained in his body, he left it embedded as it was until he received word that the Boeotians had won the battle. Once this news reached him, he said, "I have lived enough. And now I die undefeated."[239] He then pulled out the weapon in his side and rapidly expired.

10. Epaminondas never married. He was chastised for this by Pelopidas, who had a notoriously wayward son; he said Epaminondas did a disservice to his country by remaining single.[240] The great man said in response to Pelopidas, "See that you do not cause an even greater offense in producing the kind of son you have. In any case I am not wanting in progeny. The Battle of Leuctra is the legacy I leave behind as my daughter. And she will not only survive me, but will certainly live forever."

During the time that the exiles—with Pelopidas as their leader—occupied Thebes and expelled the Lacedaemonian force

---

[236] A town in the central part of the Peloponnesus. The Battle of Mantinea occurred in 362 B.C.
[237] Nepos identifies the weapon as a *sparus*, a kind of javelin that was also used as a hunting spear (*see* Oxford Latin Dict.).
[238] Nepos artfully describes how removal of the spearhead would precipitate death: *animam statim emissurum*, literally "his life-force would at once drain away."
[239] "*Satis vixi; invictus enim morior.*"
[240] By not leaving any offspring.

from the citadel, Epaminondas stayed inside his residence while the killing of civilians was taking place. Because of his unwillingness to pollute his hands with the blood of his fellow-citizens, he made no effort either to protect the wicked or to fight against them. His view was that any victory resulting from a civil war was irredeemably tainted. However, once the fighting against the Lacedaemonians broke out at the Cadmea,[241] he stood in the front ranks of the fight.

We shall have said enough of the life and virtues of this man if I may append one final point that no one will dispute. Before Epaminondas's birth, and after his death, the city of Thebes was continuously subject to the authority of other powers. Conversely, while he was in control of the city-state, Thebes remained the preeminent city in the whole of Greece. From this we may conclude that a single man was more valuable than the collective citizenry.

---

[241] The citadel at Thebes.

Epaminondas

XVI. Pelopidas [C. 410 B.C.—364 B.C.]

1. Pelopidas the Theban is more well-known to specialist historians than he is to the average person. I am not entirely sure of the best way to discuss his virtues; for if I attempt to describe his career, I may appear to be composing a general history of his times rather than a biographical sketch of the man himself. Yet if I discuss only the key events of his life, it may not be clear to those unschooled in Greek literature just how great a man he was. As far as I can, I will adapt myself to each of these considerations, and will remain mindful of my readers' lack of familiarity with the topic, as well as of the fatigue produced by reciting excessive details.

When Phoebidas the Lacedaemonian was guiding his army to Olynthus along a route through Thebes,[242] he occupied the town's citadel—which was called the Cadmea—at the prompting of a few Thebans. These Thebans wanted some way more easily to resist an adversary faction, and so aligned themselves with Lacedaemonian interests. Phoebidas, however, acted on his own; he had received no official authorization for his decision. The result of this rash step was that the Lacedaemonians removed him from command and directed him to pay a fine. Nevertheless, they declined to give the citadel back to the Thebans; they reasoned that since they had already aroused the other side's hatred, it was better to keep them under continuous pressure than to liberate them.

---

[242] In 382 B.C. Olynthus was a town in Macedonia near the modern Gulf of Kassandra.

After the Peloponnesian War and the defeat of Athens, they saw the Thebans as potential challengers to their regional dominance, and considered them the only power that might try to oppose their designs. With this consideration in mind, the Spartans gave the most powerful positions in Thebes to their puppets, and either executed or exiled the majority of the leaders of the opposing faction. Pelopidas, whose career I have begun to record, was among these exiled individuals: he was thrown out, and lost his homeland.

2. Nearly all of these exiles made their way to Athens. They were not there to languish in inactivity, but to struggle to recover their country at the first opportunity that fate might see fit to grant them. Thus once it seemed that the time for taking action had arrived—and coordinating jointly with those Thebans who shared their views—they agreed on a day to overthrow their enemies and liberate Thebes. They decided on a day when the city's chief magistrates would be assembling together for a banquet.[243]

Great deeds in history have often been carried out by a relatively small number of men. But certainly never has the downfall of a power so fearsome proceeded from an origin so unassuming. For out of the many who had been exiled, twelve young men banded together in a common cause; and in all there were not more than a hundred willing to assume such risks. Yet the power of the Lacedaemonians was brought to heel by a force of such apparently negligible size. They waged war not more on the faction of their adversaries than on the Spartans—and this was during a time when the Spartans dominated all of Greece. The majestic image of Spartan power was grievously wounded by this affair; its entire edifice would soon come crashing down at the Battle of Leuctra.

These twelve men, led by Pelopidas, left Athens by day in order to reach Thebes before the evening hours. They had with them

---

[243] During the festival of Aphrodite (Aphrodesia) in 379 B.C.

hunting dogs and nets, and were dressed like rustics from the countryside so that their group would not arouse undue suspicion. They arrived at Thebes at the precise time they intended, and took up residence at the house of Charon, the man who had given them the designated day and hour.

3. At this point I would like to comment on a principle that is somewhat removed from these events. It is that *an overabundance of confidence is often attended by a terrible calamity*. For the Theban magistrates[244] were informed immediately that the exiles from Athens had arrived; yet they were so preoccupied with drinking and feasting that they never even bothered to discover what was happening. There was something else that made their utter stupidity even more obvious. A letter written by Archinus had been carried from Athens; it was addressed to one of their colleagues, a man named Archias, who was one of the most important Theban magistrates. The letter contained every detail pertaining to the exiles' return to Thebes.

Archias had been given the letter when he was reclining[245] at the banquet table, but he slid it—still sealed—under his pillow. As he did this he remarked, "I can postpone important things until tomorrow." But as the night wore on, all of these banqueting magistrates, drowsy from the consumption of wine, were killed by Pelopidas's exiles. Once this grisly task had been completed, the people were called to take up arms for the cause of liberty. And they came running not only from within the city itself, but also from the surrounding countryside, and expelled the Lacedaemonian occupation force from the citadel. They freed their country from foreign domination; some of those who had enabled the occupation of the Cadmea were executed, and others were sent into exile.

---

[244] They were called polemarchs.

[245] In classical times, banqueters would usually eat while reclining with the aid of cushions.

4. As I have pointed out above, during this turbulent time Epaminondas remained secluded at home as long as the struggle was an issue among the citizens. Thus the glory for liberating the Thebans should be especially accorded to Pelopidas, but almost all the rest of his fame was shared jointly with Epaminondas. During the Battle of Leuctra, when Epaminondas was the commanding general, Pelopidas was the leader of the special unit[246] that first shattered the Lacedaemonian phalanx. He was also present during every moment of crisis. Thus he was in command of one wing during the attack on Sparta; and in order for Messene to be restored more quickly, he set out for Persia as an envoy.[247] In the final analysis, he was one of the two most important figures in Thebes; and even though he happened to occupy second place, he was still next to Epaminondas.

5. He was nevertheless vexed by hostile fortune. As I have already discussed, he was at first forced into exile and deprived of his country. When he wanted to bring Thessaly under Theban control and thought he would be safeguarded by the laws pertaining to diplomats (since this was the sacred rule among all nations), he was seized with Ismenias by the tyrant Alexander of Pherae and thrown into prison.[248] Epaminondas recovered him, then launched a war against Alexander. After these events, Pelopidas became permanently alienated from the man who had dishonored him.

He therefore convinced the Thebans to go to Thessaly and assist in the expulsion of its tyrants.[249] When he had been appointed supreme commander in that war and had departed with his army, he did not hesitate to engage the enemy as soon as he saw them.

---

[246] The so-called Sacred Band.

[247] Pelopidas went to Persia in 367 B.C. The Persian king Artaxerxes Mnemon wanted Messene to be restored to independence.

[248] 368 B.C. Alexander ruled Thessaly as a tyrant. Ismenias was a prominent politician in Thebes.

[249] 364 B.C. The "tyrants" referred to are probably Alexander's local appointees.

In this battle he became consumed with rage as soon as he laid eyes on Alexander. Pelopidas commanded his mount to rush towards his intended target, and moved too far away from his own men; and, hit by a barrage of enemy javelins, he was cut down. This incident took place at the very time that victory was at hand, for the forces of the tyrants had already begun to crumble. For this great feat all the states of Thessaly awarded the slain Pelopidas golden crowns and bronze statues, and bestowed a large amount of land on his children.

XVII. Agesilaus [C. 445 B.C.—359 B.C.]

1. Agesilaus the Lacedaemonian was held in high regard not only by the general consensus of historians, but in particular by Xenophon,[250] the protégé of Socrates and his especially close friend. The first noteworthy event he was involved in was a dispute over royal power with Leotychides, the son of his brother. There was a Lacedaemonian tradition, inherited from their ancestors, that they should always have two kings—who more reigned than actually ruled—coming from the two families of Procles and Eurysthenes. They were the earliest kings of Sparta, and descended from the progeny of Hercules. It was not permitted for someone from one family to become king in place of someone from the other family; this practice guaranteed that each family preserved its place in the line of succession. Primary eligibility was given to the first-born male child of the king who had died in power; but if the deceased had no male issue, then his closest familial relation was selected.

King Agis, the brother of Agesilaus, died[251] and left a son named Leotychides. Agis had not claimed the boy as his progeny when he was born, but as he lay dying, he did confirm the son as his own. This son claimed the crown for himself in opposition to his uncle Agesilaus, but he did not get what he wanted. For Agesilaus was the more favored candidate; he enjoyed the endorsement

---

[250] The Greek historian and philosopher Xenophon (c. 431 B.C.—354 B.C.) wrote a short biographical sketch of Agesilaus's life which is still extant.
[251] 398 B.C.

of Lysander, who, as we have previously noted, was politically astute and wielded considerable influence at that time.

2. As soon as he had attained power, he convinced the Lacedaemonians to send an army to Asia and commence military operations against the Persian king, reasoning that it would be better to fight him on Asian soil than in Europe. Information had been trickling out that Artaxerxes was preparing a fleet and infantry forces to send to Greece. As soon as he was given the authority to respond, Agesilaus moved with such speed that he landed in Asia[252] with his forces before the king's satraps knew he was coming. This meant that he caught all of them unprepared and oblivious to what was happening.

When Tissaphernes—who wielded ultimate authority among the king's prefects—learned of Agesilaus's incursion, he sought an armistice from the Laconian, pretending that he wanted to mediate the dispute between the Lacedaemonians and the king. His real intention was to buy time to prepare his forces; yet he was able to secure a three-month suspension of hostilities. Both sides swore they would scrupulously adhere to the pact.

Agesilaus honored his commitment with the greatest attentiveness. Tissaphernes, on the other hand, was concerned only with preparing for a renewal of hostilities. Although the Laconian was aware of the game that was being played, he nevertheless observed the truce, and said that adhering to it provided him numerous benefits. With his observable bad faith, Tissaphernes would alienate many men from his cause and provoke the angry gods against him; while he, by honoring the sacred rituals, would fortify the morale of his army, since his men would believe that they were the beneficiaries of divine will. Men would also be more likely to support them, since they usually incline towards those whom they see honoring their agreements.

---

[252] 396 B.C.

Since the barbarian had many residences in Caria, and the region at that time was considered extremely rich, Agesilaus thought that the enemy's main attack would be focused there once the armistice period expired. So he positioned all his forces in that vicinity. Yet Agesilaus directed his attention towards Phrygia and pillaged the region before Tissaphernes could move against him. With his soldiers satisfied with the large quantity of plunder accumulated, he led his army back to Ephesus for the winter; there he set up workshops to produce weapons and began his war preparations in earnest. To encourage his weapons makers to work more diligently and decorate their wares more creatively, he would give bonuses to those artisans who distinguished themselves with their industriousness. He did the same thing when it came to the different training exercises for his men: to those soldiers who distinguished themselves from their peers, Agesilaus offered generous monetary incentives. With these methods he produced a military force that was exceptionally well-trained and impressively armed.[253]

When he thought that the time had come to bring his forces out of their winter encampment, he realized that if he publicly stated in advance his intended line of march, the enemy would not believe him. They would simply occupy other regions with their forces, never doubting that Agesilaus would act differently from his stated intentions. Thus when he announced he would make a move on Sardis, Tissaphernes once again thought he should protect Caria. And when he turned out to be wrong and realized he had been duped, his attempt to come to his people's aid was too late: by the time he arrived there, Agesilaus had already fought engagements in many places and had acquired substantial plunder.

Because the Laconian understood that his adversary's cavalry was better than his, he never committed his combat power on level

---

[253] A fine sentence, worthy of Sallust: *His igitur rebus effecit ut et ornatissimum et exercitatissimum haberet exercitum.*

ground, preferring instead to engage in locations where infantry had the advantage. Thus he routed much greater enemy forces whenever he joined battle; and his operations in Asia were so adroit that the consensus of opinion judged Agesilaus to be the prevailing party.

4. He was giving serious consideration to mounting a campaign in Persia against the king himself, when a messenger sent by the ephors back home informed him[254] that the Athenians and Boeotians had declared war against the Lacedaemonians. Hearing this news, he had no other option but to return home. With this decision, one must admire his sense of duty no less than his military virtue; for although he was commanding a successful army and had supreme faith in his ability to defeat the Persian kingdom, he possessed enough self-restraint to follow orders from the absent magistrates—just as if he were a private citizen in Sparta appearing before an assembly. I only wish our own generals could have behaved in similar fashion![255] But let us continue our narrative.

---

[254] 394 B.C.

[255] A rare moment of emotion. Nepos is referring to Rome's disobedient generals who served their own interests, men like Sulla, Caesar, Antony, and Octavian.

An early nineteenth century country scene in Greece

Agesilaus placed his personal integrity ahead of the allure of the most opulent kingdom; he believed that yielding to the traditions of his country was far more glorious than imposing his will on Asia through war. With this purpose in mind he brought his forces across the Hellespont with such rapidity that he finished in thirty days a journey that had taken Xerxes a full year. When he got closer to the Peloponnesus, the Athenians, Boeotians, and their allies tried to intercept him at Coronea,[256] but he routed all of them in a decisive engagement.

The most meritorious aspect of that battle was the following. Many of the fleeing soldiers had taken refuge in the temple of Minerva. Although Agesilaus had been wounded in the battle and was angered at those who had chosen to fight him, he set aside his resentment when he was asked what he wanted done with the fugitives. He respected the sanctity of religion and ordered that they should not be harmed. Greece was not the only place where he considered temples inviolate; in barbarian lands he also showed careful deference to their altars and devotional images. The fact that those who harmed sanctuary-seeking suppliants were not viewed as sacrilegious themselves was, he declared, truly astonishing; he was also surprised that those who disrespected religious observances[257] were not more rigorously punished than those who stole from temples.

5. After this battle the locus of the entire war became the region around Corinth; for this reason, it would eventually become known as the Corinthian war. Here, under the command of Agesilaus, ten thousand of the enemy were killed in one battle; as a result, the combat power of his opponents was seen as seriously

---

[256] This was the Battle of Coronea in 394 B.C., an engagement in the Corinthian War.

[257] The phrase used is *qui religionem minuerent*, which is open to some interpretation. The verb *minuere* can mean to impede, impair, or diminish; and *religio* in this context indicates religious rites or obligation. The phrase indicates those who disrespect religious rituals.

degraded.[258] So foreign to his mind was any hint of insolence produced by glory that he truly pitied the fate of Greece, because many good men had pointlessly died as a result of his adversaries' follies. If saner heads had prevailed, he believed, a force of Greeks this size would have been able to deliver the Persians a decisive blow.

When he had forced his enemies back inside their city walls and many advisors were suggesting he assault Corinth itself, he took the position that doing this was contrary to military virtue. He said he was a man who forced transgressors to return to their responsibilities, not a man who would sack the noblest of all Greek cities. "For if," he asserted, "we are willing to destroy those who stood with us against the barbarians, we will successively destroy ourselves while foreign enemies quietly watch it happen. And at that point, they will pounce on us without any trouble whenever they want."

6. At the same time the Lacedaemonians were visited by that calamity at Leuctra.[259] Although he was pressed by many to participate, he declined to go; it was as if he had been foretold the result, and so chose to stand aside. When Epaminondas assaulted Sparta[260] and the city was without walls, he so proved his ability as a general that it was obvious to everyone that, had he not been in charge, Sparta would have been utterly destroyed. In that crisis it was his speed of decision-making that preserved the city's security.

Some youths who were terrified at the approach of the enemy wanted to defect to the Thebans, and occupied an elevation outside the city. Agesilaus, who understood how pernicious it would be if anyone in Sparta noticed that there was a group trying to

---

[258] Also known as the Battle of Nemea (394 B.C.). Agesilaus was not present at this battle: he was still returning from Asia.
[259] The Battle of Leuctra in 371 B.C.
[260] 369 B.C.

desert to the enemy, visited the location with his men and complimented the youths on their decision to take possession of the spot. He played along with the fiction that the youths had occupied the position with good intentions, and said he had also believed it was a tactical necessity. Thus he won the youths over to his side with this empty flattery, and left the location secure by augmenting it with some of his own men. When the number of those uninvolved in the desertion scheme was increased, the actual conspirators dared not start any trouble; indeed they gladly behaved themselves because they thought their original purpose had remained hidden.[261]

7. After the battle of Leuctra the Lacedaemonians without doubt never rebuilt or recovered their former power; and at the same time, Agesilaus never stopped trying to help his country with whatever resources were available to him. For when the Lacedaemonians were in particular need of financial aid, he provided assistance to all those who had rebelled against the king; and when he received a large contribution from them, he used it to help the country. One of his most admirable qualities was that although significant monies were given to him by kings, rulers, and foreign nations, he never kept anything for himself personally and never departed from standard Laconian lifestyle or dress.[262] He was satisfied with the house that had been occupied by Eurysthenes, the founder of his family line. A visitor to his residence could see no sign of extravagance or evidence of luxury; on the contrary, there was much that attested to his asceticism and restraint. In fact his house was constructed no differently from the residence of any private citizen of modest resources.

---

[261] This sentence is problematic in the original but Nepos's intended meaning is clear.

[262] The original here is elegant: *quod nihil umquam domum suam contulit, nihil de victu, nihil de vestitu Laconum mutavit*. The first part literally states that he "never took anything [i.e., financial gifts] home" with him.

8. While Nature had gifted this outstanding man in her allocation of his mental abilities, she was decidedly less benevolent in the construction of his physical form; for he was of modest height, of meager build, and burdened with a deformed foot. These shortcomings brought him more than a little disapprobation. Those who evaluated his appearance without knowing him personally tended to form a negative first impression; but those who knew his virtues could not venerate him enough.

This truth was affirmed when he traveled abroad at the age of eighty to provide assistance to Tachos[263] in Egypt. There he was reclining to eat with his men at the sea-shore—with nothing over his head, and using as a couch some straw scattered on the ground covered only with an animal hide—and all of his comrades stretched out beside him in humble and frayed clothing. They were not dressed in a way that might divulge the fact that one of them was a king; an observer would only conclude that they were in no way prosperous.

When the news of Agesilaus's arrival was reported to the king's men, gifts of all types were speedily carried to him. When they asked about Agesilaus, they could hardly believe he was one of those who was then eating. And when they presented him with the gifts they had brought in the king's name, he declined everything except the calf's meat[264] and some victuals urgently needed at that time. He gave the aromatic oils, crowns, and sweets to his servants, and ordered the remainder to be given back. The barbarians looked down on him even more after this incident, since they

---

[263] An Egyptian pharaoh of the 30th Dynasty who reigned about 361 B.C. to 359 B.C. Tachos (or Teos) sought Agesilaus's help for a military expedition against the Persians in Palestine and Phoenicia.
[264] *Vitulina*. Translating this as "veal" here seemed too suggestive of a restaurant scene.

thought his actions were due to a primitive ignorance of high-quality goods.[265]

When Agesilaus was traveling home from Egypt—after King Nectenebis had given him two hundred and twenty talents as a gift to the Spartan people—he contracted an illness and died during his arrival at the port known as Menelaus, which is located between Cyrene[266] and Egypt. In order that Agesilaus's remains might more easily be transported to Sparta, his friends coated his body with wax, as honey[267] was not available. In this way they returned him to his homeland.

---

[265] Nepos is certainly correct. Lavish gift-giving was (and is) an eastern custom, and the Persians would not have been impressed with a foreign ruler's asceticism. It would have been better for Agesilaus to distribute the gifts after the king's emissaries had left.
[266] A city on the North African coast in what is now Libya.
[267] Honey (along with other ingredients) was sometimes used as an embalming agent.

XVIII. Eumenes [C. 362 B.C.—316 B.C.]

1. Eumenes of Cardia.[268] If his virtue had received the benefit of good fortune, he would certainly not have been greater than he was, since we evaluate great men by their characters and not by their fortune; yet he would have been more well-known, and certainly more highly esteemed. His career coincided with the era in which Macedonian power flourished. As Eumenes was living among the Macedonians, it was a significant handicap for him to have been the citizen of a foreign state; for he lacked nothing except an aristocratic pedigree. He had the highest status in his own nation, but the Macedonians were resentful that he was at times valued more than they were. They nevertheless accepted this situation because he was superior to them in conscientiousness, vigilance, patience, shrewdness, and quickness of mind.

As a young man he earned the friendship of Philip, son of Amyntas. Within a short time he rose to a close familiarity with him. The innate quality of his virtue shone brightly even when he was a youth. Philip therefore kept him close at hand as a personal secretary,[269] a job that carries more prestige with the Greeks than with the Romans. We Romans view scribes[270] as little more than

---

[268] Cardia was the main town of the Thracian Chersonese (the Gallipoli peninsula). It was located at the head of the modern Gulf of Saros.

[269] *Scriba*, a scribe, clerk, or administrative assistant.

[270] Scribes and copyists were often slaves in Rome, or workers paid by the number of lines in a manuscript. *See* Houston, G.W., *Inside Roman Libraries*, Chapel Hill: Univ. of North Carolina Press (2014), pp. 14-20. Copyists were

wage-earners (which they are); but in Greece, on the other hand, no one is given this responsibility unless he is a man of good background, verified integrity, and confirmed diligence, since he is made privy to all of his leader's deliberations.

Eumenes held this position of friendship with Philip for seven years. After Philip was killed,[271] he occupied the same position with Alexander for thirteen years.[272] During the end of this time period he was placed in charge of one of the cavalry squadrons called "The Companions."[273] His counsel was always sought by both kings, and he was involved in all of the decision-making.

2. At the time of Alexander's death in Babylon, his kingdom was divided among his close comrades. The ultimate protective responsibility was delegated to Perdiccas, to whom the dying Macedonian king had bequeathed his signet ring. From this everyone concluded that he had made Perdiccas the heir to his domain until Alexander's own children reached a suitable age. Indeed Craterus and Antipater were absent at the time—and both of them were considered better choices than Perdiccas. Hephaestion was dead, and it was unquestionably true that he was the man Alexander most esteemed. At that time Eumenes was given Cappadocia—or rather pledged to him, as it was then under enemy control. Perdiccas worked very hard to earn his support; for he was aware of his loyalty and industry, and was certain that if he could gain his confidence, Eumenes would be of great use to him in implementing his goals.

---

no more prestigious in Greece than they were in Rome. Nepos is perhaps forgetting the significant difference between a lowly scribe and a king's personal secretary.

[271] Philip was king of Macedon from 359 B.C. to 336 B.C.

[272] Alexander ruled for only twelve years and eight months. Nepos counts partial years as "years."

[273] *Hetaeria* means brotherhood or society, but Nepos is referring to a specific Greek term, ἑταῖροι. This word describes the elite Macedonian shock cavalry unit "The Companions."

Perdiccas was contemplating what nearly everyone who wields great power contemplates: to take everyone else's holdings and join them together as one. Neither was he the only one who nursed this aspiration—all the rest of Alexander's associates were thinking along precisely the same lines. Leonnatus first prepared to seize Macedonia. By dangling many extravagant promises in front of Eumenes, he tried to persuade him to break with Perdiccas and form an alliance with him. When he was unable to seduce him to his plans, Perdiccas tried to have Eumenes assassinated; and he would certainly have done so had Eumenes not quietly slipped away from his guards at night.

3. At the same time, those wars[274] of unparalleled ferocity erupted which took place after Alexander's death: and all the contenders joined forces to attack Perdiccas. Although Eumenes was conscious of Perdiccas's vulnerability in being forced to contend alone with all the others, he nevertheless did not abandon his friend, and did not prefer safety over loyalty to him. Perdiccas had put him in charge of that part of Asia situated between the Taurus mountains and the Hellespont, and had positioned him there alone to oppose his adversaries in Europe. He himself had set out for Egypt to fight Ptolemy.

Eumenes had forces that were neither large in size nor especially combat-ready, since they were untrained and new to military life. Word was also circulating that Antipater and Craterus—men distinguished by their stature and experience in war—had crossed the Hellespont with a large Macedonian force. At that time Macedonian soldiers had the same level of prestige that now attaches to those of Rome, since those who hold sway over the entire world have always been viewed as the mightiest. Eumenes was well aware that if his men knew whom they would be confronting, they

---

[274] After Alexander's death, his successors fought each other for control of his vast empire. These wars are called the "Wars of the Diadochi" (Πόλεμοι τῶν Διαδόχων), and they lasted from 322 B.C. to 275 B.C.

would not only refuse to march, but would desert immediately upon hearing the news.

Thus it appeared most prudent to lead his men through secluded routes where they would not hear the truth of what was happening, and to persuade them that their objective was some random group of barbarians. He successfully adhered to this purpose. Eumenes's army was arranged in formation and had begun to fight even before his men knew the identity of the enemy force they were facing. By occupying his preferred ground before the enemy deployed, he could advantageously fight with his cavalry (which was superior) instead of having to rely on his infantry (which was decidedly less effective).

4. The battle between the two sides raged furiously for the greater part of a day. The leader Craterus was slain, as was Neoptolemus, who held the second-place position in the chain of command. Eumenes fought personally against Neoptolemus. When the two of them were locked in struggle and fell off their horses to the ground, it was obvious that there was personal animus between them, and that their fight was powered more by spirit than body; for they could not be pulled apart until one of them had drawn his last breath. Eumenes had received a few slashing wounds, but he did not withdraw from the battle: in fact he pressed the enemy even harder. After the enemy's cavalry was destroyed, their leader Craterus was cut down, and many prisoners were taken (including a number of nobles), their infantry force was baited into a location where it could not escape without Eumenes's agreement. They asked for a truce; but when Eumenes granted it, they broke their word and scuttled back to Antipater as soon as they could.

Eumenes made every effort to administer aid to Craterus, who had been carried half-dead from the battlefield. When it was clear that nothing could be done, he made sure that Craterus received a prominent funeral and arranged to have his ashes sent to his wife and children in Macedonia. For he was mindful of their former friendship—the two of them had been close during Alexander's lifetime—as well as Craterus's standing as a leader.

5. While these things were happening at the Hellespont, Perdiccas was killed near the river Nile by Antigenes and Seleucus.[275] The one who emerged triumphant from this outcome was Antipater. Those who had not supported him were sentenced to death *in absentia* by his army's vote—and among them was Eumenes. This was a heavy burden to bear, but he refused to let it defeat him or hamper his prosecution of the war; but his meager assets, while not shattering his resolve, nevertheless dampened it. Antigonus hunted him; he had a numerical advantage in all types of forces, and often tormented him with hit-and-run attacks on the march, but he was never able to confront Eumenes openly except in places where a small force could effectively contend with a larger one. Although he could not be outmaneuvered by ruses, Eumenes was eventually encircled by a much larger force. He nevertheless extricated himself from this trap with the loss of many men, and escaped to a fortress in Phrygia named Nora.

Eumenes found himself blockaded in this redoubt, and worried that his horses might lose their effectiveness due to the lack of space for physical activity. Yet he developed an ingenious method by which a standing pack animal could be warmed and exercised, so that it would more willingly take food and not suffer physical decline through muscular atrophy. He elevated the front part of the animal's body with a leather strap so that it was just barely able to touch the ground with its front legs, then with the use of a whip forced it to jump forward and kick out its hind legs.[276] This motion produced no less sweat than if the animal were running in an open space. The result of this innovation was that—to everyone's amazement—the animals were brought out of

---

[275] This was in 321 B.C.

[276] The animal handlers must have used several wide straps or some kind of supportive harness.

the fortress after a blockade of several months in as strong a physical condition as if they had been roaming in open fields.

During this siege Eumenes burned some of Antigonus's equipment and fortifications, and toppled over others as he pleased. He also stayed in one place as long as the winter months endured, since he was unable to set up camp in the open air. Spring eventually approached. Making the enemy believe he wished to give up, he then tricked Antigonus's commanders by slipping away while surrender terms were being negotiated, and got away without losing a single man.

6. Alexander's mother Olympias had sent a letter and messengers to Eumenes in Asia, seeking his counsel on whether she should go to Macedon and make a bid for power there. Her residence at that time was Epirus. He strongly discouraged her from attempting this, recommending instead that she wait until Alexander's son became king; but if she possessed an unshakeable desire for the Macedonian throne, she should forget all her injustices and not carry out any acts of retribution against anyone. Olympias did neither of these things. She went to Macedonia and there governed with unmitigated severity.

She then begged the absent Eumenes not to permit the implacable foes of Philip's house and family to kill off his issue, but to render assistance to Alexander's children. If he would do what she requested, he would first have to outfit military forces and bring them to her aid. To facilitate this enterprise, she dispatched letters to all the remaining loyal governors requesting that they submit to Eumenes and abide by his commands. He was strongly influenced by these pleas; and he thought it better, if events were in the hands of fortune, to perish while reciprocating good deeds done to him, than to stay alive by behaving as an ingrate.

7. So he gathered his forces together and made preparations for a conflict with Antigonus. With him were a number of Macedonian nobles, including Peucestes, who had been responsible for Alexander's personal security before acting as military governor

of Persia. Also present was Antigenes, commander of the Macedonian phalanx. Eumenes was concerned about the growth of resentment—which of course was unavoidable—if he himself as a foreigner held the position of supreme commander, instead of one of the large number of Macedonians who were with him. He erected a tent in Alexander's name at the army's headquarters, and ordered that a golden throne with scepter and diadem be placed inside it.[277]

Everyone, he said, should convene there on a daily basis to hold discussions on the most critical issues. Eumenes believed he could minimize any festering animosity towards himself if he appeared to conduct the war with just the facade of personal command, and utilized as much as possible the cohesive prestige of Alexander's name. This policy worked: for their meetings and deliberations were held not at Eumenes's headquarters, but at Alexander's headquarters. To a large degree Eumenes succeeded in deflecting attention away from himself, while continuing to make sure that he had the final say in everything.

8. He clashed with Antigonus at Paraetacae,[278] not in regular battle formation, but on the march; Eumenes inflicted serious damage on him, forcing him to retreat to Media to spend the winter. He then divided up his forces within the borders of Persia for the winter—not as he wanted, but according to the wishes of his men. For the celebrated phalanx of Alexander the Great, which had marched in incomparable triumph over Asia and had brought Persia to its knees, was now well-acquainted with glory and accustomed to license. Unsatisfied with showing obedience to its commanders, it proposed instead to command them, just as our own military veterans do in the present era.[279]

Thus there is a great danger that our military men will behave in the same manner as the Macedonian generals, and destroy everything through their lack of restraint and self-serving outlawry—

---

[277] In order to evoke the memory and authority of Alexander.
[278] In 317 B.C.
[279] Another reference to the insubordinate Roman generals of Nepos's era.

not just those who oppose them, but even the accomplices who aid them in their plans. Anyone who reads about the actions of the Macedonian veterans of that era will detect unmistakable similarities with the events of our own time, and will understand that the only real difference is the intervening gulf of years. But let me resume my narrative of the generals of that time.[280]

They selected their winter quarters not on the basis of military utility, but instead on its capacity to support their pleasures. The various units were also separated from each other by long distances. Antigonus knew he could not contend with his enemies when they were prepared to fight: so when he learned of the disposition of their forces, he realized he had to come up with a new way to deal with them.

There were two roads coming from Media—where Antigonus's encampment was located—to the winter quarters of his enemy. The shorter road passed through desert terrain that was devoid of inhabitants due to its lack of water, and it took about ten days to traverse. The other road was twice as long and more meandering, but was plentiful in resources and overflowing with everything a traveler might need. If he picked the circuitous road, he knew his enemies would learn about his approach before he was even a third of the way there; but if he chose the arid desert route, he hoped to overwhelm an unsuspecting enemy.

He issued orders to get ready for the march. The men collected as many water bladders and leather sacks as they could find, fodder for the animals, and enough cooked food to last ten days so that camp fires could be kept to an absolute minimum. Antigonus did not disclose his intended route to anyone. Having made his preparations, he set out along the road he had committed himself to.

9. Antigonus was almost halfway to his destination when smoke from his camp alerted Eumenes that an enemy force might

---

[280] This striking paragraph shows Nepos at his very best.

be on its way.²⁸¹ Eumenes then convened a meeting with his commanders to solicit opinions on the correct course of action. Everyone knew that their own forces could not be drawn up quickly enough to defend against the approaching enemy. When the officers began to waver and showed signs of desperation, Eumenes told them that if they moved quickly and carried out his instructions—which they had previously failed to do—he would handle the situation. For while the enemy still needed five days to complete their desert crossing, he would take action to hold them up for at least another five days; for this reason, his commanders should go around and get their men ready for action.

Eumenes crafted the following stratagem to delay the advance of Antigonus. He sent reliable men to the lowest part of those mountains that happened to be in the enemy's path; he instructed them to light bonfires as soon as night began over the most widely dispersed area possible, and gradually diminish them during the second watch.²⁸² In the third watch they should let the fires die down to a low level. By replicating the standard watch procedures used in a military camp, Eumenes's goal was to fool the enemy into thinking that he had encamped there, and that Antigonus's march through the desert had been discovered. He told his men to repeat this same trick the next night.

The men who had been assigned this special mission carried it out faithfully. Antigonus saw the fires once daylight faded, and concluded that his presence in the area was now known. His enemies, he was sure, had brought their forces there to confront him. So he changed his plan. Believing he could not attack them without the element of surprise, he diverted his line of march and picked the longer, more circuitous road with abundant resources. Seeking to improve the army's fighting condition, Antigonus halted in place for a day to rest the men and animals.

10. So did Eumenes thwart a cunning opponent and impede his offensive movement. He did not, however, benefit much from

---

[281] The men apparently disobeyed his orders not to light fires.
[282] *Secunda vigilia*. Night watches were divided into four shifts.

this. As a consequence of malice from the other commanders and the naked perfidy of the Macedonian veterans, Eumenes was betrayed to Antigonus even after having been successful in battle. This happened despite the fact that on three previous occasions the army had sworn to protect him and never abandon him. Yet some of them were so pathetically deficient in virtue that they preferred to ignore their duty of loyalty rather than to stand by him.

Antigonus, despite being Eumenes's sworn antagonist, might still have saved him if his own officers had allowed it; he understood that no one else could be as valuable to him for the looming conflicts everyone knew were taking shape. For Seleucus, Lysimachus, and Ptolemy—all of whom wielded considerable power—were arrayed against Antigonus, and he would have to fight them for the top position. But the men around Antigonus could not stomach a settlement between the two commanders; for these officers knew that if Eumenes and Antigonus resolved their differences, they themselves would be reduced to comparative insignificance. Antigonus himself was also seething with anger, to the extent that only the most ambitious expectations of maximalist outcomes could satisfy him.

11. Once Eumenes was taken into custody, the commander of the detachment holding him asked Antigonus how he wanted his prisoner to be watched over. Antigonus's response was, "Like you were guarding the most cunning of lions, or the most aggressive of elephants." At this point he was still trying to decide whether to spare his life or put him to death.

Two types of visitors came to see Eumenes: those who wanted to feed their hatred by gloating over his abject humiliation, and those who, because of their long personal friendship, wanted to talk with him and raise his spirits. There were also many who were genuinely curious about his personal appearance and wanted to take the measure of this man they had so long and so emphatically feared, this formidable figure whose personal ruin had been their only hope of victory.

But once Eumenes had been in prison for some time, he told Onomarchus (who was the head officer of the guards) that he was amazed he had been kept in custody for three days. He said it was not becoming of Antigonus's usual good sense to behave so disgracefully towards a defeated opponent. He wanted to know why he had been neither executed nor released from custody. Onomachus thought this kind of talk was insolent, and shot back, "What? If this is how you see it, why didn't you die in battle instead of allowing yourself to be taken prisoner?" Eumenes replied, "I really do wish that had happened. The only reason why it didn't was because I've never come to grips with anyone stronger than myself. I've never crossed swords with anyone who did not submit to me." And this statement was no lie: for it was not an enemy's military prowess that had defeated him, but the treachery of his friends.[283]...For he had a command presence that conveyed authority, an unrivaled endurance in tolerating burdens, and a bodily frame that was not so much massive as it was athletic.

12. Antigonus, not daring to make the decision alone on what to do with Eumenes, decided to consult with his colleagues. Everyone was initially confused; they could not fathom why a man who had tormented them so much, and for so many years, had not already been put to death. Eumenes had often brought them to the brink of hopelessness, and had wiped out their best commanders; he was the only man who could endanger their security so long as he remained alive. They knew his death would end a persistent threat. If Antigonus ultimately spared Eumenes's life, they asked, who would stand shoulder to shoulder with him as a friend? For they made it clear to Antigonus that they would not serve with him if Eumenes entered the picture.

Once Antigonus learned of the council's ruling, he struggled with his conscience and delayed making a final decision for six days. Because he was worried about the possibility of a mutiny in

---

[283] There is apparently a lacuna in the text here.

the army, he would not let anyone to see Eumenes in custody, and ordered that his prisoner's daily food ration be terminated. He would not, he declared, shed the blood of a man who had once been his friend. But Eumenes did not experience the bite of hunger for more than two days, at which time he was throttled[284] by his guards; the killing took place while the camp was being moved, and it was done without Antigonus's knowledge.

13. So came the death of Eumenes at the age of forty-five, after having served Philip for seven years[285] from the time he was twenty, as we noted earlier, and having held the same position with Alexander the Great for thirteen years. He was the commander of a cavalry unit for a year during this period; and after Alexander's death he was in charge of an army. Of the very best enemy generals, there were some he outfought, and some he killed. His death was due not to Antigonus's fighting prowess, but was a result of his shabby betrayal by the Macedonians. How highly he was regarded by all those who claimed the throne after Alexander's death, we can clearly see from the fact that while Eumenes was alive no one but him was actually *called* king, only prefect.

After his death these same people took power and began calling themselves kings; but none of them kept up the pretense, widely intoned by all of them at first, that they were holding power as custodians for the benefit of Alexander's children. But

---

[284] The exact method of Eumenes's killing seems ambiguous. The verb used is *iugulare*, which according to the Oxford Latin Dictionary can mean to kill by cutting the throat, to kill by other violent means, or (figuratively) to destroy a person or a cause. Death by strangulation would be consistent with Antigonus's stated desire not to shed Eumenes's blood. It was also common for high-status captives in ancient times (e.g., the philosopher Boethius) to be dispatched by strangulation, as it was considered more "humane" than the use of the sword. Yet the use of the word *iugulare* alone, without additional explanation, may not rule out other execution methods.

[285] This "seven years" refers to the sentence near the end of chapter 1 stating that Eumenes "held this position of friendship with Philip for seven years."

once their most formidable rival had been eliminated, the remaining contenders showed their true faces. The conspirators in this evil affair were Antigonus, Ptolemy, Seleucus, Lysimacus, and Cassander.[286]

Yet Antigonus sent Eumenes's remains to his relatives for a proper burial. He was accorded the funerary rites worthy of a soldier and a man of distinction, and the entire army appeared for the ceremony. And they took care to deliver his remains[287] to his mother, wife, and children in Cappadocia.

---

[286] Alexander's children were killed in the power struggles that followed.
[287] The word used is *ossa* or bones, but a too literal translation would convey a crude tone. His body was cremated: the ashes were buried, but the bones would have been delivered to his family.

XIX. Phocion [C. 402 B.C.—C. 318 B.C.]

1. Phocion of Athens. Although he was often in charge of armies and occupied the highest civil positions, he was nevertheless more noted for the integrity with which he lived his life, than for his achievements in military affairs. Thus while there is no memory of his campaigns, his integrity achieved celebrated status and was crowned with the appellation of "The Good." Throughout his life his financial condition remained very modest. Yet he could have made himself extremely wealthy as a result of the frequent public positions and high powers conferred on him by the people. When he once turned down a huge monetary gift from King Philip, the king's emissaries encouraged him to take it, pointing out that even though he himself might not need such pecuniary inducements, he should think about the interests of his children, who would be hard-pressed to uphold their father's prestige if burdened with limited resources. Phocion's response to them was: "If they follow my example, they will maintain this small plot of land which has guided me to my current station in life. But if they follow a path different from mine, I do not want their extravagance to be nourished and enlarged at the cost of my reputation."

2. Until nearly his eightieth year he had enjoyed the benefits of good fortune; but as his final years approached, he incurred the implacable wrath of his fellow-citizens. This was firstly because he had approved of Demades's plan to deliver the city over to Antipater; another reason was that it was through his urging that Demosthenes and the others who were believed to have served

their country well were banished by public decree.[288] His behavior had given offense not only because his advice harmed his country's interests, but also because he had betrayed the trust of a friend. Phocion owed his public position to the favor and support of Demosthenes, who had come to his aid in the struggle against Chares. Demosthenes had also defended him—and acquitted him—several times when he was facing capital charges. Phocion not only failed to stand up for the great orator in his hour of need, but he actively worked to bring about his downfall.

His ultimate ruin, however, was the result of one particular transgression that took place during the time he held by popular consent the position of greatest power. He was warned by Dercylus that a prefect of Cassander[289] named Nicanor was scheming to take the Piraeus of the Athenians. He was also advised to make sure that the state was not denied critical supplies. The public heard Phocion deny that there was any such danger—and he assured everyone that the issue was his responsibility. Shortly after this assurance, Nicanor gained control of the Piraeus, without which Athens cannot survive at all. When the people agreed that it should be forcibly retaken, he not only failed to summon anyone to arms, but showed no desire to lead them even after they had become armed.

3. At that time in Athens there were two political factions: one advocated on behalf of the people, and the other supported the aristocracy. Phocion and Demetrius of Phalerum belonged to the

---

[288] The issues were complex, but basically the sequence of events was as follows. In 322 B.C. Antipater of Macedon defeated a Greek coalition at Cranon in Thessaly. Demades and Phocion were sent by the Athenians to negotiate with Antipater. Some concessions to Antipater were made that Phocion then asked him to waive. He did not. Demosthenes, who was strongly anti-Macedonian, was forced to flee Athens and was later sentenced to death. Phocion did what he could to protect his city, but it is unavoidable that a domestic leader serving under foreign occupation will acquire some taint of collaboration.

[289] Cassander was the son of Antipater. He succeeded his father in 319 B.C.

party of the upper classes. Both of these factions enjoyed the protection of the Macedonians; for the populists favored Polyperchon, while the sympathies of the aristocrats were with Cassander. At this time Cassander was forced out of Macedonia by Polyperchon. The result of this was that the people—who were now in a more powerful position—immediately condemned the leaders of the opposing faction and ran them out of the country,[290] including Phocion and Demetrius of Phalerum. As an additional step they then sent emissaries to Polyperchon, asking him to confirm their decisions. Phocion also decided to see Polyperchon. Once he arrived he was ordered to explain his position to King Philip; but in fact he pled his case to Polyperchon (who was then in charge of such official matters). Phocion was accused by Hagnon of abandoning the Piraeus to Nicanor, and was then taken into custody by a ruling of the council. He was then transferred to Athens to stand trial according to the laws of the city.

4. When he arrived there, he was transported by carriage because his advanced years prevented him from walking about on his own. A large crowd had formed to see him. Some of the citizens, recalling his departed fame, felt sympathy for him in his fragile senescence; the majority of them, however, were afire with hatred due to their suspicion that he had committed treason with regard to the Piraeus. They also resented the fact that in his old age he had stood against the people's interests. For this reason he was not afforded the chance to speak in his own defense, or to argue the merits of his case.

Once the required legal formalities had been completed, he was sentenced by the tribunal and then handed over to the Eleven,[291] who according to Athenian custom are responsible for administering punishment to those convicted of crimes. As he was

---

[290] I.e., out of Athens.
[291] *Undecimvires*. The "Eleven" was a municipal board in Athens that was responsible for the punishment of criminals.

led to his death, a man named Euphiletus, who had once been a close friend, approached him. As tears filled his eyes, Euphiletus said, "Oh, what an injustice you are being subjected to, Phocion!" The statesman responded, "It was not unforeseen. The majority of Athens's great men have suffered this same fate." The public's loathing for him was so great that no free man dared to bury him. And for this reason he was buried by slaves.[292]

---

[292] He was first buried in Megaris, since those convicted of treason could not be buried within Attica. His remains were later moved back to Athens, however.

XX. Timoleon [C. 411 B.C.—337 B.C.]

1. Timoleon the Corinthian. By all accounts this man incontestably demonstrated greatness. For he—and I firmly believe he alone—was fated to shoulder the burden of liberating the country that birthed him from a tyrant's domination, and to remove the yoke of longstanding servitude from the Syracusans, whom he had been sent to assist. He alone, simply by virtue of his arrival there, was granted the honor of restoring the whole of Sicily to its original condition after many years of vexatious wars and barbarian[293] oppression.

But while these events were taking place, he was forced to contend with an inconstant fortune. And he accomplished something that is considered extremely difficult: he proved to be wiser in times of good fortune than in times of hardship. When his brother Timophanes (whom the Corinthians had picked as leader) seized power as a tyrant with the help of mercenaries, he took the position that adhering to the rule of law was more important than ruling over his country. And despite the fact that he could have participated in his brother's power grab, he was so far removed from complicity in this crime that he was more worried about the freedom of his fellow-citizens than about his brother's personal safety. With these concerns in mind, he arranged for his tyrant brother to be assassinated with the help of a diviner[294] and a common relative, namely, the man married to the sister they had in common.

---

[293] Apparently referring to the Carthaginians, who had controlled parts of Sicily.
[294] A *haruspex*, a soothsayer who makes predictions by reading the entrails of animals.

Timoleon not only did no violence to Timophanes, but he had no desire even to look at his brother's blood. For while the killing was taking place, he was away from the scene setting up a secure perimeter, so that none of the tyrant's attendants could take action to help him. This highly commendable action was not looked upon favorably by all, however; there were some who thought he had committed a grave offense against familial loyalty and, motivated by jealousy, had stained with dishonor the fruits of his courage. After this deed, his mother would not allow him to enter her household; whenever she saw Timoleon thereafter, she would call him a wicked fratricide and utter curses against him. This bitterness and hatred so disturbed him that at times he thought of committing suicide, so as to leave behind the society of ungrateful men by seeking death's somber kingdom.

2. Meanwhile, Dionysius was again able to wield power over the Syracusans after Dion had been killed there. Dionysius's enemies petitioned Corinth for aid, asking for someone who could serve as a war leader. The man they sent was Timoleon; and with incredible good luck he entirely expelled Dionysius from Sicily.[295] Although Timoleon could have had him killed, this was not his intention; he permitted the tyrant to arrive in Corinth unharmed. Both rulers who bore the name Dionysius had often used their resources to help Corinth in the past, and he wanted to preserve the memory of this generosity. He also thought that the most memorable victory was a triumph characterized more by clemency than by retribution. He wanted people to appreciate the pathetic state to which he had reduced Dionysius, this tyrant who had once strutted about so arrogantly from the heights of power, and he wanted them to see this with their own eyes, rather than just hear about it.

Timoleon went to war with Hicetas after Dionysius was gone. Hicetas had once been a political enemy of Dionysius. But his opposition to the deposed ruler had been based not on a principled

---

[295] In 344 B.C.

objection to tyranny, but on a desire to hold supreme power himself. Proof of this was shown when Hicetas declined to relinquish power once Dionysius had been expelled. After Timoleon defeated Hicetas,[296] he crushed a huge force of Carthaginians at the river Crinissus,[297] and forced them to accept the reality that, after occupying Sicily for so many years, they would now have to content themselves with being allowed to hold Africa. He also captured a bellicose and powerful Italian commander named Mamercus who had come to Sicily to give the tyrants military assistance.

3. Once these events had taken place, he realized that because of the war's extended length not only the provinces, but also the cities, were depopulated. So he first collected as many local people as he could, then brought in settlers from Corinth, since Syracuse had originally been founded by Corinthians. He gave the original citizens back what had belonged to them, and to the new arrivals he parceled out tracts of land that had been abandoned as a consequence of the war. He restored the smashed walls of the cities and the abandoned temples, and returned to the various political entities their laws and freedoms. From a truly devastating war Timoleon restored such tranquility to the entire island that he, and not the people who had originally established these cities, was thereafter looked upon as their founder.

He broke apart from its foundations the citadel of Syracuse, a structure that the tyrant had fortified to maintain control over the city. Desiring that the fewest possible vestiges of servitude should remain, he pulled down the tyrant's other fortifications as well. Although he possessed the means to rule Sicily without the consent of its inhabitants, and although the people so venerated him that he could have secured power with no dissenting voices, his

---

[296] In 339 B.C.

[297] The river is also spelled Crimissus. The Battle of the Crimissus was fought in early June 339 B.C. between Timoleon and a Carthaginian army led by Hamilcar and Asdrubal.

preference was to be loved instead of feared. Thus at the first opportunity he relinquished power and lived out his remaining years as a private citizen of Syracuse. This was certainly a well-considered decision, for his benevolence then gave him the authority that other rulers could only hope to acquire by becoming kings. He became the recipient of every public honor; and from that point no official action was taken at Syracuse without first seeking Timoleon's counsel on the matter. Not only was no one else's opinion given priority over his, but no other opinion was even debated; and this was more due to prudence than favor.

Sixteenth century woodcut of Timoleon

4. Despite not having any disease, he lost his eyesight when he became elderly. He bore this burden with such even temper that no one ever heard him complain about it, nor did he pursue his public and private activities with any diminished intensity as a result of it. Indeed he even came to the theater when the people's assembly was in session there. Because of his condition he was brought there by two harnessed mules; and from this vehicle he would then pronounce his views. No one attributed this behavior to haughtiness, for he never uttered anything that was either insolent or conceited. Indeed when he heard himself publicly lauded, he never said anything except that he was extremely grateful to the gods for selecting him as the leader most capable of carrying out their design of restoring Sicily's freedom. He was convinced that every event in human affairs took place in accordance with the will of the gods; and in his house he set up a shrine to Automatia[298] which he honored with the utmost piety.

5. Incredible occurrences of good fortune augmented the sublime virtuousness of this man. For all his crucial battles took place on his birthday, and for this reason all of Sicily marked that day as a festival. On one occasion a belligerent and unappreciative man named Laphystius tried to have him served with a lawsuit[299] in order to litigate some alleged issue. Many people then joined together to squelch the insolence of this man by physical force. Timoleon asked the crowd to leave the man alone. He reminded them that he himself had endured the greatest struggles and the most extreme dangers just so that this man Laphystius, or some

---

[298] A surname for Tyche, the Greek goddess of fortune. The usage is very rare, but attested: *Automatia vero fortuna est, cui quum benefacta omnia referret accepta Timoleon, domi Automatiae sacellum extruxit: quod significat Aemilius Probus*, etc. (*Ludovici Caelii Rhodigini Lectionum Antiquarum Libri Triginta*, Frankfurt: Apud heredes Andreae Wecheli, Claudium Marnium, & Ioan. Aubrium (1599), p. 304.

[299] *Vadimonium imponere*. *Vadimonium* normally means bail or surety but here signifies a summons to court.

other person, might have the ability to assert such rights. This was the splendor of liberty, he pointed out: a condition where anyone could make use of the laws for whatever purpose he or she wanted. Once in the people's assembly when a man similar to Laphystius—whose name was Demaenetus—started to criticize Timoleon's actions, and even directed verbal barbs against him personally, Timoleon said that his fondest hope had at last been delivered. For his prayer to the immortal gods had always been to restore such freedom to the Syracusans that would permit them to speak their minds on any desired subject without having to fear retribution.

When he passed away, he was interred by the Syracusans in a state funeral, and laid to rest in a gymnasium called the Timoleonteum. All of Sicily paid honor to his memory.

A 1546 woodcut from Münster's Cosmographia
showing southern Italy and Sicily

Timoleon

XXI. On Kings

1. My sketches thus far have concerned the commanders of Greek ancestry who may be considered worthy of remembrance.[300] Kings have not been included; I have felt no need to treat them here since the memorable deeds of all of them have been discussed elsewhere.[301] Nevertheless these are not very large in number.[302] Agesilaus the Lacedaemonian was a king in name, but not in authority, which was unlike the situation with other Spartan kings. But among those men who wielded actual power along with their offices, the greatest in my judgment were the Persian monarchs Cyrus[303] and Darius,[304] son of Hystaspes. Both of these men were private citizens who arrived at power through strength of character.

Cyrus was killed in battle in the country of the Messagetae,[305] while Darius expired in old age. Besides these two, there are three

---

[300] Datames and Eumenes were not of Greek ancestry, but Nepos is painting with broad strokes to make his point.

[301] As discussed in the introduction, Nepos wrote a large work on noteworthy men (*De Viris Illustribus*), of which one part (probably the first book) dealt specifically with kings of foreign nations.

[302] *Neque tamen ii admodum sunt multi.* Meaning that there are not many men who were both kings and military commanders.

[303] Cyrus the Great (c. 600 B.C.—530 B.C.).

[304] Darius the Great (c. 550 B.C.—486 B.C.), the son of Hystaspes and the grandson of Arsames.

[305] Described by Herodotus (I.214).

other kings of the same nationality worthy of note: Xerxes[306] and the two kings who used the name Artaxerxes, that is, Artaxerxes Macrochir[307] and Artaxerxes Mnemon.[308] Xerxes's greatest notoriety derives from the fact that he waged war against Greece by land and sea using the largest armies in historical memory. But Macrochir's fame rests principally on his distinguished and handsome physical form, an advantage he augmented considerably by his bravery in battle, since no other Persian was stronger than he in the art of fighting. On the other hand, Mnemon achieved prominence for his sense of justice; for when he lost his wife due to the wickedness of his mother,[309] he vented his sorrow in a way that evinced the disciplined restraint of filial piety.[310] Out of these kings just mentioned, the two who bore the same name[311] paid their dues to nature with terminal diseases, while the third[312] was assassinated by his prefect Artabanus.[313]

---

[306] Xerxes I (519 B.C.—465 B.C.). The Messagetae were a central Asian people inhabiting roughly the region of modern Turkmenistan and western Uzbekistan.

[307] Artaxerxes I Macrochir ("The Long-Handed") ruled from 465 B.C.—424 B.C.

[308] Artaxerxes II Mnemon ("The Remembering") ruled from 404 B.C.—358 B.C.

[309] Mnemon's wife Stateira, the daughter of Persian nobleman Hydarnes, was poisoned around 400 B.C. by Mnemon's mother Parysatis. *See* Plutarch, *Artaxerxes* 17-19.

[310] I.e., his traditional sense of filial respect restrained him from punishing his mother with extreme severity: *tantum indulsit dolori, ut eum pietas vinceret.* Literally, "he indulged his sorrow in such a way that filial piety still controlled him." The bonds of obligation to one's parents were stronger in the ancient world than now, and had a religious backing. His mother was exiled, not executed.

[311] Artaxerxes Macrochir and Artaxerxes Mnemon.

[312] Xerxes.

[313] Artabanus was commander of the royal bodyguard. He and an accomplice (a eunuch named Aspamitres) murdered Xerxes in August 465 B.C.

2. As for Macedon, two kings stand out over all the others when it comes to the glory of their achievements: Philip, the son of Amyntas, and Alexander the Great. One of these expired from sickness at Babylon;[314] and Philip was killed by Pausanias at Aegiae near the theater when he was on his way to watch the performances. Also noteworthy was Pyrrhus, one of the kings of Epirus, who waged war against the Roman people.[315] When he was assaulting the city of Argos in the Peloponnesus, he died from having been struck by a stone.

Significant also was the first Dionysius, a Sicilian king.[316] He was skilled in feats of arms and experienced in war, and almost never indulged in sexual wantonness, luxury, or greed—a personal trait not often encountered in a tyrant. His desire was essentially focused on nothing except the exercise of complete and perpetual power. And for this reason he was inclined to cruelty; because he was fixated on maintaining control, he showed no mercy to anyone he saw as a potential threat. He attained the position of tyrant through martial virtue, but kept it through incredibly good fortune. He exceeded sixty years of age at the time of his death, and left behind a thriving kingdom. During the many years of his rule he never experienced the death of any of his issue, despite fathering children from three wives and having numerous grandchildren.

3. In addition there were among the friends of Alexander the Great many important kings who began their reigns after he died.

---

[314] The cause of Alexander's death has been disputed. It was either due to excessive drinking or (more likely) complications from his wounds in battle.
[315] Pyrrhus of Epirus (318 B.C.—272 B.C.).
[316] Dionysius I of Syracuse (c. 432 B.C.—367 B.C.).

Some of these were Antigonus and his son Demetrius, Lysimachus,[317] Seleucus,[318] and Ptolemy.[319] Antigonus was killed[320] in battle while fighting Seleucus and Lysimachus; and a similar fate visited Lysimachus when he fought Seleucus. For once their amicable relations fell apart, they began to wage war against each other. Demetrius gave his daughter in marriage to Seleucus; however, he failed to confirm that the ties of friendship would continue between them. He was captured in war and died of an illness while in the custody of his son-in-law. Not long after this Seleucus was murdered by the guile of Ptolemaeus Ceraunus; when Ptolemaeus's father had expelled him from Alexandria and he needed help from others, Seleucus had taken him in. Yet it is said that Ptolemaeus himself was executed by his son after he turned his kingdom over to the son during his lifetime.[321]

Because I believe I have spoken enough about these kings, it will not be disagreeable to linger a bit on the lives of Hamilcar and Hannibal, who, in brilliance and greatness of soul, are universally agreed to have excelled in ability all other commanders born in Africa.

---

[317] Lysimachus (c. 360 B.C.—281 B.C.). Alexander's successors were called *diadochi*.
[318] Seleucus I Nicator (c. 359 B.C.—281 B.C.). He was assassinated near Thrace by Ptolemy Keraunos.
[319] Ptolemy I Soter (c. 367 B.C.—282 B.C.), the founder of the Ptolemaic dynasty that ruled Egypt for three hundred years until the death of Cleopatra.
[320] In 301 B.C.
[321] This is not correct. Ptolemy Keraunos (*keraunos* meaning "thunderbolt" in Greek) was king of Macedon from 281 to 279 B.C. He was actually captured and killed by a Gaulish leader named Bolgius. Nepos seems to be confusing Ptolemy Keraunos with different kings bearing the name Ptolemy. Ptolemy I Soter gave his kingdom to his son Ptolemy Philadelphus, but he was certainly not killed by his son. Ptolemy III Euergetes (reigned 246 B.C.—222 B.C.) may or may not have been killed by his degenerate son Ptolemy IV Philopator (reigned 221 B.C.—204 B.C.). Ptolemy IV seems to have arranged his mother's murder, which took place at the outset of his reign.

1546 woodcut from Münster's Cosmographia *showing a fortified town. Note the hapless figure in the left foreground.*

XXII. Hamilcar [C. 275 B.C.—228 B.C.]

1. Hamilcar the Carthaginian, the son of Hannibal, and bearing the family name Barca.³²² Towards the end of the First Punic War,³²³ he began to lead an army in Sicily while still practically a youth.³²⁴ Before he arrived in Sicily the progress of the war for the Carthaginians was unsatisfactory on land and sea; but once he appeared on the scene, he never retreated from the enemy nor gave them an opportunity to inflict damage. Quite the contrary: when presented with an opportunity, he engaged them, and always emerged the victor. And this was not all. When the Carthaginians had lost nearly all their holdings in Sicily, he so stoutly defended Eryx³²⁵ that it almost seemed as if the surrounding area had been untouched by war. Meanwhile the Carthaginians, once they had been bested by the fleet of Roman consul Caius Lutatius³²⁶ near the Aegates Islands,³²⁷ resolved to end the war and gave Hamilcar permission to hold peace talks.

Despite his intense desire to wage war, he nevertheless believed he should serve the cause of peace; for he understood his

---

³²² The Barcid family was a distinguished one of old Carthage, and many of its members held important positions. The Semitic root of the word indicates "lightning" (e.g., the Arabic برق or *barq*).
³²³ The First Punic War lasted from 264 B.C. to 241 B.C.
³²⁴ He assumed command in 247 B.C.
³²⁵ A fortified town in the western part of the island.
³²⁶ Caius Lutatius Catulus was actually proconsul. The battle took place in 241 B.C.
³²⁷ Islands off the west coast of Sicily.

country had exhausted its resources and could no longer bear the hardships of protracted conflict. Yet his mind soon formed the desire to resume military operations once conditions had improved a bit, and to press the Romans until his men either conquered through superior prowess or went down in complete defeat. He worked toward peace with this ultimate goal in mind. He was so unyielding during the peace talks that when Catulus said he would not bring an end to hostilities until all those who occupied Eryx laid down their weapons and left Sicily, he answered that he would prefer to see his country lie in ruins, and he himself meet death, rather than return to Carthage cloaked in such dishonor. For it was not consistent with his concept of martial virtue to turn over the weapons he had been given by his country that were supposed to be used against her enemies. Faced with Hamilcar's intractability, Catulus finally relented.

2. Yet when he arrived in Carthage he realized that the republic's situation was quite different from what he had expected. For protracted military disasters abroad had provoked such domestic conflict that Carthage was never in comparable peril until the time of the state's destruction. The first crisis was that the mercenary troops who had been hired to fight Rome—twenty thousand of them in all—had mutinied. They encouraged all of Africa[328] to join their uprising, and made an assault on Carthage itself. The Carthaginians were so terrified by these ominous developments that they sought help from the Romans. This assistance they procured. Eventually, however, after they had reached the outer limits of desperation, they put Hamilcar in command.[329]

Although there were now over one hundred thousand armed men to contend with, Hamilcar not only expelled the enemy from Carthage's walls, but he was able to trap them in narrow terrain;

---

[328] In classical times the term "Africa" meant what we today call "North Africa."

[329] This turmoil lasted from 241 B.C. to 238 B.C. Hamilcar was given command in 239 B.C.

so neutralized, more of them died of hunger than by combat. All the seditious towns—including Utica and Hippo, the most robust in all of Africa—he returned to Carthage's control. Yet he did not rest here; he enlarged the boundaries of Carthaginian control, and imposed such tranquility over the whole of Africa that there seemed to have been no war in this region for many years.

3. He carried through these intentions in accordance with his wishes. Then, consumed with hatred for the Romans and animated by confidence in his abilities, he arranged to be sent to Spain as commander of an army, so that he might more easily find an excuse to initiate hostilities. He brought his young son Hannibal with him, who was then nine years old. With him also was an illustrious and handsome youth named Hasdrubal, whom some said was favorably regarded by Hamilcar in a way that was inappropriate. A man of his stature, however, could never be without vicious accusers.[330] Due to this allegation, the prefect of morals[331] would not permit the youth to be with Hamilcar. The general responded by giving Hasdrubal his daughter in marriage, for according to the custom of his people, a father-in-law and son-in-law could not be prevented from associating with each other.

I have made mention of Hasdrubal because when Hamilcar was killed, he was in charge of the army and achieved many great things; but he was the first one to subvert, using bribery as his tool, the morals of the Carthaginians. And after Hasdrubal's death,[332] Hannibal rose to the position of army commander.

4. But once Hamilcar crossed the sea and arrived in Spain, he

---

[330] Nepos wisely discounts this rumor, which is certainly slander. Hamilcar (like his son Hannibal) had enemies not just among the Romans, but among competing political factions in his native Carthage. Both of these groups of enemies had an interest in spreading such malicious stories.

[331] Apparently a civil office in Carthage regulating public morals.

[332] Hasdrubal commanded in Spain from 229 B.C. to 221 B.C. He was assassinated in 221 B.C. by a slave of the Celtic king Tagus. Hannibal was then proclaimed commander of the army.

accomplished many great things through the beneficial intervention of fortune. He brought to heel many powerful and bellicose peoples and enabled all Africa to benefit from an inflow of horses, arms, men, and money. When he was forming plans to conduct military operations in Italy—and nine years after he had arrived in Spain—he was killed in battle while fighting the Vettones.[333] It was his unrelenting hostility towards Rome that appears to have been the primary origin of the second Punic war; for his son Hannibal was so motivated by his father's unremitting pleas[334] that he preferred to die rather than miss his opportunity to confront the Romans.

---

[333] A Celtiberian people of western Spain. They inhabited an area roughly where the Spanish provinces of Salamanca and Ávila are today.
[334] I.e., pleas to attack Rome.

Hamilcar Barca

XXIII. Hannibal [C. 247 B.C.—C. 182 B.C.]

1. Hannibal the Carthaginian, the son of Hamilcar. If it is true (and no one doubts that it is true) that the Roman people have shown themselves to be superior to all other peoples in martial virtue, then no one can deny that Hannibal surpassed all other military commanders in ability to the same extent that the Roman people outstripped all other peoples in fortitude. For every time he battled with the Romans in Italy, he always emerged as the winner. And had he not been deprived of his full potential by the jealousy of his own people at home, it seems he would have been able to defeat the Romans. But the malice of the mob crippled the valor of one great man. He so cultivated what could be called an inherited hatred of Rome, traceable to his father, that he would sooner have died than set it aside. Even after he had been forced to leave his country and had to subsist on the generosity of foreigners, he never stopped fighting the Romans in spirit.

2. For he not only enlisted Philip,[335] who was a long distance away, as an enemy of Rome; he did the very same thing with Antiochus,[336] who was the most powerful king of that era. Antiochus became so consumed with a desire for war that he tried to prepare a campaign in Italy all the way from the Red Sea.

---

[335] Philip V of Macedon (238 B.C.—179 B.C.). He entered into a treaty with Hannibal in 215 B.C.

[336] Antiochus III of Syria (c. 241 B.C.—187 B.C.). He unsuccessfully tried to resist the rising power of Rome, fighting a four year war against her beginning in 192 B.C.

Roman envoys came to Antiochus to discover his purposes and attempt, using clandestine manipulations, to arouse the king's suspicions of Hannibal; they implied they had bribed him to change his original plans. To some extent these schemes worked. Hannibal saw what was happening and perceived that he was being cut off from the king's more sensitive deliberations. When the moment was right, he went to the king and pointed out the many instances of his loyalty and his hostility towards Rome. He told him this: "When I was a little boy not more than nine years old, my father Hamilcar, as he was leaving for Spain as a commander, sacrificed some animals in Carthage to Jupiter, the best and most important god. While this ritual was taking place, he asked me if I wanted to accompany him on this expedition. I accepted this offer with pleasure and started to beg him not to have second thoughts about bringing me. He then said, 'I will do it, as long as you swear to do what I ask.' He then led me to the altar where he had performed the sacrifices. He cleared everyone else away, had me place my hands on the altar, and ordered me to swear that I would never be friends with Rome. From that time until the present day, I have so upheld the sanctity of this oath given to my father that no one should doubt I will continue to honor it in the future. So if you are thinking of becoming friends with the Romans, it would be better not to share that with me. But when you prepare for war, your plans will not amount to anything unless you put me in command."

A conference of notables from Münster's Cosmographia *(1546)*

3. Thus he set out for Spain with his father at the age I previously noted. After Hamilcar died, and Hasdrubal replaced him as commander, Hannibal was put in charge of the cavalry units. When Hasdrubal himself died, the army selected Hannibal as the new supreme commander. When news of Hannibal's selection reached Carthage, the decision was publicly ratified; thus Hannibal was elevated to command when he was less than twenty-five years old. Over the next three years, he brought all the various Spanish tribes under Carthaginian control by application of military force; he took Saguntum[337] by siege, a city confederated with Rome; and he formed three large armies. One of these armies he sent to Africa; the second he sent to his brother Hasdrubal in Spain; and the third he himself led into Italy. He crossed the Pyrenees mountain range.[338] Wherever he went he clashed with the local inhabitants, and defeated anyone who opposed him.

He then reached the Alps, the range that separates Italy from Gaul which no one before him had ever crossed with an army except the Grecian Hercules—which is why that area is called the 'Grecian Pass.' He crushed the Alpine peoples who tried to prevent his passage, made the region accessible, constructed roads, and so improved movement in the area that a fully equipped elephant was able to go where previously a single unarmed man had barely been able to crawl. By such methods he led his forces through the Alps and entered Italy.

4. At the Rhone he had clashed with the consul Publius Cornelius Scipio, and had put him to flight.[339] He fought the same consul at Clastidium[340] and the Po, wounded him, and chased his forces away. At the Trebia[341] this same Scipio, along with his colleague Tiberius Longus, confronted him a third time; he engaged

---

[337] The modern city of Murviedro.
[338] This was in 218 B.C.
[339] Scipio was not actually present.
[340] Modern Casteggio, which is a bit south of the Po.
[341] Modern Trebbia.

them both and demolished them. He then moved through Liguria over the Apennines and headed for Etruria. During this movement he was stricken by such a serious eye ailment that he never fully regained vision in his right eye thereafter. As Hannibal was still trying to deal with this problem and was being carried around in a litter, he crushed the consul Caius Flaminius with his army at Trasimene[342] and killed him. The same thing happened to the praetor Caius Centenius not too long after this, as he was occupying a strategic pass with a selected group of men.

He then came to Apulia. There he faced two consuls, Caius Terentius and Lucius Aemilius, both of whom he shattered in a single engagement.[343] The consul Paulus was killed, along with a few other former consuls, among them Gnaeus Servilius Geminus, who had been consul the previous year.

5. Hannibal now faced no opposition after having fought this battle, and proceeded to march on Rome itself.[344] He paused in the hills located near the city; after encamping there for several days, he headed back to Capua[345] and was confronted by the Roman dictator Quintus Fabius Maximus in the vicinity of Falernum.[346] Finding himself enclosed in a narrow passage, Hannibal maneuvered his way out by night without any human losses to his army, and thus managed to outfox Fabius, a highly experienced general. For during the night Hannibal had his men tie

---

[342] A lake in the modern province of Perugia. The Battle of Lake Trasimene (fought in June 217 B.C.) is considered the largest ambush in history.

[343] This was the famous Battle of Cannae, one of history's greatest battles, where the Roman forces were annihilated in a double envelopment. It was fought in August 216 B.C.

[344] In fact Hannibal did not immediately march on Rome after the Cannae victory. He delayed for a long time, probably because he had not expected such rapid progress in Italy, and needed additional men and siege engines to mount an assault on the city. Yet he never received adequate support from the Carthaginian authorities.

[345] The capital of Campania.

[346] A region in west Campania.

bundles of sticks to the horns of cattle, which were then set on fire; he then sent a large number of them to run around here and there with horns ablaze. The unexpected arrival of this bizarre sight inspired such fear in the Roman army that not a single man dared to go outside the camp's fortifications.

A few days after this event, Hannibal baited into battle Marcus Minucius Rufus (the master of horse whose authority equaled that of the dictator) using trickery, and completely routed him. Even while absent from the battlefield, Hannibal was able to lure Tiberius Sempronius Gracchus (who had been consul two times) into an ambush in Lucania and destroy him. Using the same tactic, he killed Marcus Claudius Marcellus at Venusia[347] during his fifth term of office as consul.

We would need a great deal of space to recount all his battles. It will be enough, then, simply to mention this one fact to appreciate just how brilliant a commander Hannibal was: as long as he remained in Italy, no one could stand against him in battle. And after the battle of Cannae, no one dared set up camp near him in an exposed area.

6. Still undefeated, he was recalled to defend his country, and there continued the war against Publius Scipio—the son of the Scipio whom he had defeated first at the Rhone, then again at the Po, and a third time at the Trebia. Since Carthage's fighting capability was now depleted, Hannibal desired to suspend hostilities in the hope of renewing them later under more favorable circumstances. He conducted truce talks with Scipio, but they could not reach a comprehensive agreement. A few days after their meeting, he fought with Scipio at Zama and—it is hardly believable to say—lost the battle.[348] He arrived at Hadrumentum after a day and two nights, a town that was about three hundred miles from Zama. During this escape, the Numidians who had fled with Hannibal

---

[347] A town in west Apulia, modern Venosa.
[348] The Battle of Zama was fought in 202 B.C.

from the battlefield treacherously rebelled against him; he not only evaded them, but annihilated them. At Hadrumentum he reorganized the remainder of the soldiers who had retreated from Zama, and after a massive recruitment effort, he assembled many new units in a few days.

Hannibal

7. While Hannibal was occupied with these efforts, the Carthaginians brought the war with the Romans to an end.[349] Yet he remained at the head of the army even after this, and continued to pursue his designs in Africa until the consulship of Publius Sulpicius and Caius Aurelius. During the magistracies of these two men, Carthaginian envoys arrived in Rome to thank the senate and the Roman people for making peace with them. In support of their mission, they gave the Roman senate a golden crown and asked for their hostages to be relocated to Fregellae.[350]

They also asked for the return of their prisoners of war. The official response of the senate to the Carthaginian envoys was this: their gift was gratefully accepted; the hostages would be relocated to the place requested by the envoys; the prisoners would not be returned because Hannibal—whose actions had initiated the war and remained implacably opposed to Rome—was still in charge of the army, together with his brother Mago. Once the Carthaginians heard this response, they summoned Hannibal and Mago to Carthage. After having held the office of praetor[351] for twenty-one years, Hannibal was made a king[352] when he returned to the city. Just as with Roman consuls, in Carthage two kings were selected every year to serve a one-year term.

In this magistracy Hannibal showed the same level of diligence that he had displayed in war. For he levied taxes that not only allowed the Romans to be paid according to the peace agreement, but also were substantial enough to permit something to be added to the treasury. During the consulship of Marcus Claudius

---

[349] The peace treaty was concluded in 201 B.C.
[350] Modern Ceprano.
[351] Nepos is somewhat confusingly using Roman terms to describe foreign offices. One of the duties of a Roman praetor was command of an army, and this is what Nepos means: that Hannibal had been a general for twenty-one years.
[352] The actual Punic name for this office was *suffes*. It was not a monarch, but some kind of magistrate.

and Lucius Furius, legates from Rome came to Carthage. Hannibal thought they were sent to request that he be taken into custody; so before they had a chance to address the Carthaginian senate, he boarded a ship in secret and fled to King Antiochus in Syria. When this news leaked out, the Carthaginians dispatched two ships to arrest him if they could intercept his vessel. They then confiscated his property, razed his house to its foundations, and branded him a fugitive.

8. But in the third year after he had fled his homeland, Hannibal landed in the district of Cyrene in Africa with five ships during the consulship of Lucius Cornelius and Quintus Minucius. His goal was to see if the Carthaginians might be persuaded to fight Rome with the expectation of help from King Antiochus, whom Hannibal had by then induced to land in Italy with his armies. He also sent his brother Mago to Italy. When the Carthaginians became aware of this, they imposed the same punishment on the absent Mago that they had imposed on his brother. Now faced with a desperate situation, the two brothers readied their ships and put to sea, and Hannibal eventually reached Antiochus. With regard to the death of Mago, however, two different accounts have been given: some say he met his end in a shipwreck, while others relate that he was murdered by his own slaves.

And if Antiochus had chosen to follow Hannibal's guidance in prosecuting the war with the same enthusiasm that he had resolved to enter it, he would have battled for supreme power at a place closer to the Tiber, rather than at Thermopylae.[353] Although Hannibal saw that the king was not handling his campaign competently, he still never abandoned him in his design. He commanded a few ships which he had been ordered to sail from Syria to Asia; and with these ships he fought a Rhodian fleet in

---

[353] Antiochus was defeated at Thermopylae in 191 B.C. by Marcus Acilius Glabrio.

the Pamphylian Sea. In this fight he was overcome by his adversary's larger numbers, but he prevailed in the sector of battle where he was personally conducting operations.

9. Once Antiochus had lost, Hannibal feared he would be turned over to the Romans—and without doubt this would have happened had he given his enemies the chance. He went to the Gortynians[354] in Crete, where he could try to decide his next move. Being the extremely astute man that he was, he sensed he would be in real peril unless he devised some way to deal with the greed of the Cretans; for he was carrying a large amount of money with him, and he knew that this information had begun to circulate. He therefore adopted the following scheme.

He filled a number of *amphorae* with lead weights, topping them off with gold and silver. With important local citizens as witnesses, he then placed these large jars in the temple of Diana, acting as if he were permitting them to be the custodians of his wealth. Having duped them in this way, he took some bronze statues he was traveling with, filled them with all his money, and tossed them haphazardly in an open, unroofed area of his house. The Gortynians scrupulously secured the temple of Diana—not so much from the incursions of random intruders, but from Hannibal himself, to block him from accessing and removing anything from the temple without their knowing about it.

10. Having outfoxed the Cretans and kept his funds intact, the Carthaginian then traveled to see Prusias[355] in Pontus. With Prusias he maintained the same views of Italy that he always had; he was entirely occupied in arming the king and preparing his army for conflict with the Romans. When Hannibal saw that the king's resources were not exactly vast, he made friends with other local rulers and forged bonds with bellicose nations. Prusias was on poor relations with Eumenes, the Pergamese king, a close friend

---

[354] The Cretans living near Gortyna (modern Metropoli).
[355] The king of Bithynia.

of the Romans; and the two leaders had been attacking each other on land and sea. In every place, however, Eumenes was able to prevail because of his close ties with the Romans: and this was why Hannibal wanted to depose him. If he were removed, Hannibal thought, everything else would become easier for him.

He devised the following scheme to kill Eumenes. They had resolved to deploy the fleet in a few days, and the number of enemy vessels exceeded those possessed by Hannibal. He thus had to fight using deception, since the imbalance in arms was not in his favor. He ordered as many poisonous snakes as possible to be collected and placed alive in earthen containers.[356] Once a large number of these had been secured,[357] he assembled his men on the day the naval battle was to have been fought and instructed them to make a direct assault on Eumenes's flagship, while adopting a defensive posture towards the rest of the enemy's ships. Due to the large number of snakes they had, these were orders they could easily follow. Hannibal also said he would let them know which ship belonged to the king;[358] and he promised to give them a large reward for killing the king or taking him alive.

After he had given his men this incentive, the fleets of both belligerents were arranged for battle. Once the battle lines had been drawn, and before the signal to attack was given, Hannibal sent out a small boat with a courier carrying a staff[359] as a symbol of peace, so that his men could clearly see which vessel was carrying Eumenes. When this courier reached the enemy ships and displayed his letter, he declared he was looking for the king. He was immediately brought before Eumenes, since everyone assumed it was some message about peace terms. Having revealed

---

[356] *Imperavit quam plurimas venenatas serpentes vivas conligi easque in vasa fictilia conici.*
[357] An early example of the use of biological warfare.
[358] I.e., which ship was carrying Eumenes.
[359] *Caduceum*, which is defined in the Oxford Latin Dictionary as "a staff carried by heralds as a token of peace."

the enemy's flagship to his own side, the courier then returned to the vessel from which he had left.

But once Eumenes opened the letter, he saw that there was nothing in it except words of ridicule directed at him. He tried to discern the purpose behind this strange incident, but could deduce nothing; despite this, he did not hesitate to commit himself to battle immediately. During the engagement the Bithynians as a coordinated group went straight for Eumenes's vessel, just as Hannibal had ordered. The king could not fend off their attack, and tried to save himself by fleeing; and he could only accomplish this by enclosing himself within the fortified position that had been prepared on the closest shore.

When the remaining Pergamese ships began to gain the upper hand against their adversaries, suddenly the earthen containers I mentioned earlier came out and began to be thrown at them. The first salvo of these jars only provoked derisive laughter among the enemy: they could not appreciate the significance of what was happening. However, once they saw their decks swarming with venomous snakes—and paralyzed by this novel tactic because they could not evade the vipers—they abruptly turned around and headed back to their nautical camp. Thus Hannibal, using his intelligence, triumphed over the arms of the Pergamese. Neither was this the only time when this happened; for he often beat other adversaries in infantry battles using comparable cunning.

12. While these events transpired in Asia, it happened that Prusias's emissaries were eating dinner in Rome with the consul Titus Quinctius Flaminius. During the meal Hannibal's name came up, and one of the emissaries disclosed that he was in the kingdom of Prusias. The next day Flaminius relayed this information to the senate. The senators, thinking that they would have no respite from Hannibal's schemes as long as he remained alive, sent envoys (including Flaminius) to Bithynia to ask the king not to host their most implacable enemy, but instead to turn him over to the Romans. Prusias dared not deny this request; but he did insist that the Romans not force him to do anything that ran counter

to the law of hospitality. The Romans themselves could arrest Hannibal, if they could manage it; for they could easily discover where he was living. Hannibal resided in one place, a fortress which the king had given him as a gift, and he had built this structure in such a way that it had escape portals in every part of it. Clearly, he was afraid of having to endure the sequence of events that ultimately took place.

When the Roman emissaries came to Hannibal's stronghold and surrounded it with a multitude of soldiers, a young slave observing from one of the doors told Hannibal that a number of armed men—more than what one might typically see—had appeared. The general told him to check all the doors of the structure and let him know if they were similarly blocked on every other side. The slave quickly informed him of the situation, and stated that troops were posted at all avenues of escape from the building. Hannibal now knew that what was happening was deliberate, that he himself was their objective, and that he could no longer save his life. Unwilling to allow someone else to determine how he would forfeit his life, and imbued with the memory of his former martial virtue, he ingested the poison which he regularly kept with him.

13. Thus expired in his seventieth year[360] this most courageous of men, after having carried out such diverse and manifold enterprises. It is not clear during what consulship his death occurred. According to Atticus's *Annals*, Hannibal died in the consulship of Marcus Claudius Marcellus and Quintus Fabius Labeo; but Polybius dates his death at the time Lucius Aemilius Paulus and Gnaeus Baebius Tamphilus held office.[361] Sulpicius Blitho[362] places the event in the consulship of Publius Cornelius Cethegus and Marcus Baebius Tamphilus.

---

[360] His age at death was closer to sixty-five.

[361] This is the Titus Pomponius Atticus (c. 110 B.C.—32 B.C.), the friend of Cicero, whose biography appears in this volume. He wrote a Roman history that has not survived. Polybius (c. 208 B.C.—c. 125 B.C.) is one of the great Greek historians.

[362] Nothing is known of this writer.

And although his attention was devoted to such momentous wars, this great man nevertheless allotted some time to literary pursuits. Several books of his, composed in Greek, are known to exist. One of these was intended for the Rhodians, and related the exploits of Gnaeus Manlius Volso in Asia.[363] Many writers have described the military campaigns of Hannibal; among them are two comrades, Silenus and Sosylus the Lacedaemonian, who were actually with him in camp and lived alongside him so long as fortune permitted. Hannibal also made use of this Sosylus as his Greek language instructor.

It is now time for us to bring this book to a conclusion and sketch the lives of the Roman generals.[364] Comparing their respective achievements in this way[365] will more easily enable us to determine who should be judged the greater historical figure.

---

[363] What a pity that none of these works have come down to us.

[364] The book Nepos says he now intends to begin (called *De Excellentibus Ducibus Romanorum*, or *On the Great Roman Commanders*) has been lost. His intention was to compare the foreign generals in the present work with the Roman generals in this lost work.

[365] I.e., comparing the deeds of the Roman commanders with the deeds of the foreign commanders in this book.

FROM THE BOOK ON THE LATIN HISTORIANS[366]

---

[366] This biographical sketch on Cato, and the one on Atticus that follows it, are from Nepos's lost work *De Historicis Latinis* (*On the Latin Historians*).

XXIV. Cato [234 B.C.—149 B.C.]

1. Marcus Cato was born in the town of Tusculum.[367] Before applying himself to the standard Roman political career path, he lived in the Sabine region as a young man, since he owned property there inherited from his father.[368] At the urging of Lucius Valerius Flaccus—who was later Cato's colleague as consul and censor, as the former censor Marcus Perpenna[369] liked to say—he relocated to Rome and began his political career. At the age of seventeen he entered military service; and during the consulship of Quintus Fabius and Marcus Claudius, he served as tribune of the soldiers in Sicily. Returning from this assignment, he then served under Caius Claudius Nero and distinguished himself by his performance in the battle of Sena, in which Hannibal's brother Hasdrubal was killed.

When Cato became quaestor he served under the consul Publius Africanus,[370] although his professional life with him was not in strict accordance with tradition; for he constantly disagreed with him for the rest of his days.[371] He was made aedile of the plebians with Caius Helvius.[372] As praetor he maintained the

---

[367] Tusculum is in the Alban hills near Rome, and very close to the modern town of Frascati.
[368] *Quod ibi heredium a patre relictum habebat.*
[369] Marcus Perpenna (c. 147 B.C.—49 B.C.) was censor in 86 B.C. and consul in 92 B.C.
[370] The famous general Publius Cornelius Scipio Africanus, for whom Cato served as quaestor in 204 B.C. At that time Scipio was proconsul, not consul.
[371] The professional relationship was supposed to resemble a close mentorship. Perhaps two headstrong personalities like Scipio and Cato could not adjust to this kind of arrangement.
[372] In 199 B.C.

province of Sardinia. When he was leaving Africa at an earlier time as quaestor, he had brought away the poet Ennius;[373] and in my view, this act was no less magnificent than the most celebrated Sardinian military triumph.

2. He bore the consulship[374] with Lucius Valerius Flaccus. The province of Hither Spain was assigned to him by lot, and from there he brought home a triumph. When he had stayed there a considerable time, Publius Scipio Africanus—who was then in his second consulate, and in his first consulate had had Cato as his quaestor—wanted to recall Cato from the province and substitute himself in his place. Although Scipio then occupied the highest office in the land, he was still unable to get the senate to approve his plan, because the republic was at that time administered according to law rather than political interest.[375] For this reason he felt resentment towards the senate; and when he finished his term as consul, he chose to live as a private citizen in the city.

---

[373] I.e., brought him to Rome. The poet Ennius (239 B.C.—169 B.C.) is often quoted by Cicero and was famous in antiquity, but only fragments of his output have survived.
[374] In 195 B.C.
[375] There is more than a hint of bitterness in these words.

*Ruins of the amphitheater at Tusculum, the town of Cato's birth.
Photo by the translator (2018)*

But Cato, who was appointed censor with the same Flaccus, exercised his authority in that position quite sternly. For he punished several nobles, and added many new things to his edict[376] in order to control extravagance, which even then was starting to appear. From his youthful years to the end of his life—roughly eighty years in all—he never stopped attracting hostility as a result of his zealous service on behalf of the Roman republic. Although he endured the accusations of many, his methods not only failed to diminish his prestige, but his virtues grew in renown as long as he lived.

3. In all fields of endeavor he was distinguished by an exceptional level of industry; for he was accomplished in agriculture, practiced in legal matters, a great military commander, an admirable orator, and very much dedicated to literary activity. Although his literary work began when he was advanced in years, his progress was nevertheless so rapid that one cannot easily find Greek or Italian cultural subjects with which he was unacquainted. He wrote speeches from the time he was very young. He undertook the writing of history when he was very old, composing seven books in all.

The first book describes the deeds of the early Roman kings, while the second and third discuss how each of the Italic states came into being; and this was apparently the reason why he titled his work *Origines*, or *Origins*.[377] The fourth book deals with the first Punic war, and the fifth book recounts the second. All of these events are described by separate headings;[378] and he treated the remaining wars in the same way, until the time of the praetor

---

[376] The censor's edict (*edictum*) was essentially a code of regulations and rules.

[377] This would likely have been Cato's most valuable work. His treatise on agriculture, *De Agricultura*, has survived, and remains the oldest complete prose work in Latin (dating to about 160 B.C.).

[378] *Capitulatim*, meaning "in summary fashion" or "by headings."

Servius Galba, the man who devastated the Lusitanians.[379] He did not identify the generals in these wars by name, but laid out the relevant events without calling attention to specific personalities. In the same books he described remarkable events and unusual natural scenes in Italy and the two Spains.[380] His work was composed with great diligence and effort, but not specialized scholarship.

I have already said much about Cato's life and personal traits in the book I composed separately about him at the request of Titus Pomponius Atticus. For this reason, I would ask those eager to learn about Cato to consult that volume.[381]

---

[379] The praetor Servius Galba conducted massacres against the Lusitanians in 151—150 B.C. He was recalled to Rome and harshly reprimanded by Cato for his actions.

[380] Nepos's words are a bit vague here, but the meaning is clear: *In iisdem exposuit quae in Italia Hispaniisque aut fierent aut viderentur admiranda*. For the Romans there were actually two Spanish regions, *Hispania Citerior* (Hither Spain, basically the eastern coast of Spain, comprising modern Catalonia and Valencia) and *Hispania Ulterior* (Further Spain, roughly the southern coast of the Iberian peninsula).

[381] Nepos is reminding us that Cato is briefly sketched here only because he was a Latin historian. His fuller, more complete biography of Cato was in a different book which has not survived.

XXV. Atticus [C. 110 B.C.—32 B.C.]

1. Titus Pomponius Atticus,[382] whose lineage could be traced to the earliest origins of the Roman people, always kept the equestrian rank[383] he inherited from his ancestors. His father was diligent and, for that era, wealthy; he also had a high regard for literature. And just as he himself loved literary pursuits, he educated his son in all the subjects that should be imparted to young people. Besides an innate keenness of mind, the boy possessed the finest elocution and vocal tone, so that he not only quickly absorbed the literary selections he was taught, but was also able to recite them superbly. For this reason he was considered outstanding among his peers as a boy, and shone more brightly than his aristocratic schoolmates could bear with equanimity. Therefore, through his own efforts, he advanced all of them forward; among them were Lucius Torquatus,[384] Caius Marius the son,[385] and Marcus Cicero. Atticus became such close friends with all these men that, for the rest of his life, they held no one else in higher regard.

2. His father died at a young age. When Atticus himself was a young man, he did not lack for direct experience with danger, due

---

[382] He acquired the surname "Atticus" as an acknowledgment of his familiarity with Greek language and culture.
[383] Rome during the republican period had three social classes: the aristocratic (senatorial) class, the equestrian (knight) class, and the plebian class.
[384] Consul in 65 B.C.
[385] Consul in 82 B.C.

to the fact that he had a family connection by marriage with Publius Sulpicius,[386] who was killed when he was tribune of the plebs. Atticus's first cousin Anicia had married Servius, who was the brother of Sulpicius. So once Sulpicius had been slain, he thought it was the right time to pursue his interests, and left for Athens. He could see that Rome was in turmoil because of Cinna's uprising, and that he would have no chance to live in a way suitable for a man of his background without incurring the hostility of one or another political faction. For the sentiments of the Roman people were split; some lined up with Sulla's faction, and others favored Cinna.

Yet when the young Marius was condemned as an enemy, Atticus helped him with his own resources and expedited his escape by giving him money. And in order that his trip to Athens would not have an adverse impact on his personal property,[387] he brought a large portion of his wealth with him to Athens. In Greece he lived in such a way that he rightly became beloved to all the Athenians. For besides his political connections in Rome—which were extensive even as a young man—he often alleviated their public needs by contributions from his own funds.

When the authorities needed to borrow money to pay off another creditor,[388] and were unable to secure a fair offer, Atticus always helped to complete the transaction; and he never demanded usurious loan rates from them, nor permitted the repayment period to extend longer than what had been agreed. Both of these things were, of course, good for the borrowers: for he neither tolerated

---

[386] Publius Sulpicius Rufus, a famous orator executed on Sulla's orders in 88 B.C.

[387] I.e., out of fear that his property in Rome might be confiscated in his absence.

[388] The word used here is *versura* (*versuram facere*), which has no succinct equivalent in English. It indicates the borrowing from one creditor to pay off another. The Oxford Latin Dictionary defines it as "the process of exchanging one creditor for another (by borrowing to pay a debt)."

the repayment period to be dragged out through misguided leniency, nor allowed the loan balance to swell by the compounding of interest. He added another considerate gesture to this service he performed. He set up a grain distribution system for the whole populace, so that each man received six *modii* of wheat; this unit of measure is called in Athens a *medimnus*.[389]

3. Moreover, Atticus so conducted himself that he seemed to be on the same level with the humblest citizens, yet at the same time a peer of those at the very top.[390] As a natural consequence, the Athenians publicly conferred on him all the honors they could, and were even eager to make him a citizen; but this honor he did not desire, since some legal authorities have ruled that Roman citizenship is lost if one accepts it from somewhere else.

As long as he remained in Athens, he did not want to have any statue of himself raised; he could not stop this, however, once he had left. Thus the Athenians erected a few statues to Atticus and Phidias[391] in their most sacred locations, for they considered him an advocate and authority on all matters related to public administration. So it was primarily a gift of fortune that Atticus was born in that city, above all others, which was the seat of world empire, and that this city was both his country and his home. And it was a compelling testament to his good sense that, when he arrived in that city[392] which overshadowed all others in antiquity, cultural refinement, and learning, it valued him more highly than any other man.

4. When Sulla arrived in Athens as he was returning from Asia, he kept Atticus with him as long as he was in Athens, for he

---

[389] The Greek *medimnus* was apparently equal to about six Roman *modii* (one *modius* was equal to 16 *sextarii*, or a bit less than two gallons).

[390] *Hic autem sic se gerebat, ut communis infimis, par principibus videretur.*

[391] This individual is unknown. I follow the Chambers text in using "Phidias," but Ortmann omits this name entirely; and some manuscripts use "Pilia" (Atticus's wife). The reading is unclear.

[392] I.e., Athens.

was captivated by the youth's character and erudition. He had mastered Greek so thoroughly that he seemed to have been born in Athens;[393] and he was so polished in the use of Latin that one could tell his facility in the language was inborn, rather than the product of applied instruction.

He so flawlessly recited poems in Greek and Latin that not a single improvement could be made. This made Sulla want to have Atticus constantly by his side; he even wished to bring him to Rome with his entourage. When Sulla tried to get him to agree to this, Atticus said, "I ask you, please do not force me to fight those whom I declined to join in fighting you, but instead left Italy." Sulla commended the young man for his sense of responsibility, and ordered that when he left for Rome, all the gifts he had received while in Athens should be given to Atticus.

He lived in Athens for many years, devoting as much care to the maintenance of his estate as befitted a diligent head of a household. All his remaining time was given to the pursuit of letters and to Athenian public affairs. In addition to this, he performed all kinds of services for his friends in Rome: he regularly appeared during their elections, and was not absent when some important matter was being administered. He showed a remarkable degree of loyalty to Cicero during all his political dangers, even giving him two hundred and fifty thousand sesterces when he was forced to flee abroad. Once a degree of stability had returned to Rome, Cicero came back, apparently during the consulate of Lucius Cotta and Lucius Torquatus.[394] All the Athenian citizens escorted Atticus when the time came for him to leave Athens, and their tears bespoke the sadness they would experience from being deprived of him.

5. His maternal uncle was the Roman knight Quintus Caecilius, a friend of Lucius Lucullus; Caecilius was rich, but had a

---

[393] We must allow for some hyperbole here from Nepos.
[394] In 65 B.C.

nettlesome disposition. Atticus handled his uncle's dourness with such skill that, although no one else could stand him, he preserved Caecilius's benevolence without displeasing him until the old man reached an advanced age. His abilities in this regard brought certain rewards: just as Caecilius was about to die, he adopted Atticus and permitted him to inherit three-fourths of his estate. This fractional share represented about ten million sesterces.

Atticus's sister was the spouse of Quintus Tullius Cicero. The union had been devised by Marcus Cicero, with whom Atticus had lived in the closest friendship from the time they were schoolboys together. He was on much closer terms with Marcus than with Quintus Cicero; and from this fact we may conclude that when it comes to friendship, similarity of character matters more than relations formed by marriage.[395]

He also enjoyed the intimate friendship of Quintus Hortensius (who occupied the top position for eloquence in those days) to such a degree that one could not tell who loved him more, Cicero or Hortensius. As he was the common link between these two great men, he brought about something that was extremely difficult: seeing that no malicious conflict developed between the two rival orators for the highest public accolades.

6. In the republic he behaved himself in such a way that he always was, and always was considered to be, on the side of the best people. Nevertheless he did not involve himself in the vagaries of political disputes, since he believed that those who became embroiled in them had no more control over their lives than those who were thrown about by rough seas. He had no wish to seek political office, although that career option was available to him either through his popularity or his fitness for office. In the pervasive culture of corruption that existed at the time, such public

---

[395] *Ut iudicari possit plus in amicitia valere similitudinem morum quam affinitatem.* The word *affinitas* here means relations or connections formed by marriage.

positions could neither be pursued in the ways of our ancestors, nor attained while obeying the laws; and as the public morals were in an advanced state of decay, it was also not possible for an office-holder to carry out his duties to the state without danger to himself.

Frontispiece of a 1644 edition of Nepos

He never came near a public sale of property that had been confiscated.[396] He never acted as a bondsman[397] or contractor.[398] He never made an accusation against anyone, either in his own name or as a signatory[399] on behalf of someone else. He never pursued a legal action on some matter related to his own property, nor did he ever have a trial.[400] He accepted the prefectures[401] offered to him by various consuls and praetors, on the condition that he not follow any of them into his province. He was content to receive the honor, and had no interest in adding to his wealth. He did not even want to go with Quintus Cicero to Asia, even though he could have obtained the office of deputy[402] under him: he did not think it was appropriate to be a praetor's deputy after he had turned down the job of praetor. By doing this, he was not only trying to maintain his integrity, but also his mental tranquility, since his decision would remove even the appearance of any misconduct. The outcome was that everyone appreciated his observations even more, since they could see that Atticus was motivated by a sense of duty, not by fear or hope.

7. Caesar's civil war began when Atticus was about sixty years old.[403] He made use of the fact that his age removed him

---

[396] Property confiscated from proscribed persons was sold at public auction. Buying such property was considered a disreputable practice, and those who did so were known as *sectores*.

[397] *Praes* indicates "a person who acts as a surety or security (for the payment or fulfilment of a contract or obligation)." *Oxf. Lat. Dict.*

[398] *Manceps* is a contractor or agent of the public revenue. The point of the sentence is to show that Atticus played no part in extracting money from citizens.

[399] *Subscribens*, or adding a supporting signature to an indictment.

[400] Lawsuits were brought before a praetor, who would then appoint a judge (*iudex*) to oversee the case. Atticus never wished to be embroiled in such matters, whether as litigant or judge.

[401] I.e., the command, or office, of *praefectus*.

[402] The word used is *legatus*, which can mean a general's assistant, or a provincial governor's assistant.

[403] In 49 B.C.

from military service, and made no effort to leave the city. Out of his own estate, Atticus provided his friends with whatever they needed when they went to join Pompey's army. He never antagonized Pompey, who knew him; and he had accepted no favors from him, unlike others who had enriched themselves by taking jobs or money from Pompey. Some of these men joined his army only begrudgingly, while others deeply offended the general by staying at home.[404] Atticus's unwillingness to take sides in the war was so appreciated by Caesar that when he emerged the winner, and was writing letters to notable citizens asking for financial contributions, Caesar not only refused to bother Atticus, but also pardoned his sister's son and Quintus Cicero, who were from Pompey's camp. Thus, by making use of his lifelong policy,[405] he avoided new dangers.

8. After the assassination of Caesar, there was a subsequent period of time in which the republic looked like it was controlled by Cassius and the Brutuses;[406] the entire country seemed to be aligned with their side. The nature of Atticus's friendship with Marcus Brutus was such that Brutus had more intimacy with the older gentleman[407] than with any other of Brutus's own age; not only did he make Atticus his most important counsellor, he also developed a close friendship with him.

Some men had floated a plan for the knights to set up a special fund for Caesar's assassins, and they thought this could easily be done if the major figures in that order would supply the funding. A man named Caius Flavius, one of Brutus's friends, asked Atticus if he wanted to take the lead in this scheme. Atticus thought it was better to help one's friends than to get involved in factions, and he had always tried to steer clear of such agreements. So he

---

[404] I.e., not joining his army at all.
[405] Meaning his policy of preserving his independence, while not antagonizing powerful men.
[406] I.e., Decimus Brutus and Marcus Brutus.
[407] Atticus at the time was 65, and Brutus was 34.

told Brutus that if he, Brutus, wanted to make use of his financial resources, he could use as much as was available; but that he would not meet with any third party about it, nor would he discuss the issue with anyone else. Thus, the general consensus on this issue was shut down by Atticus's lone dissenting voice.

Not long after this Antony started to gain ascendancy. Brutus and Cassius abandoned the responsibilities of office given them by the consul[408] as a formality and, in desperation, went into exile.[409] Atticus, who had refused to give money with the others when the faction seemed successful, sent one hundred thousand sesterces as a gift to Brutus when he had been deposed and was leaving Italy. Atticus even ordered that an additional three hundred thousand be sent to Brutus when he was in Epirus. Yet he did not try to ingratiate himself with Antony's power, nor abandon those who were desperate.

9. The war's progress brought it eventually to Mutina.[410] If I were to say that he displayed wisdom during this time, I would be praising him less than I should. For it was more like he was divinely inspired, if we may use the term "divine inspiration" to describe a continuous natural goodness that remains both unaffected and undiminished by every external circumstance. Once Antony was declared an outlaw, he left Italy, and there was no prospect of his being restored to power. Antony's friends were attacked not only by his enemies (who by this time were powerful and plentiful), but even by those who threw in their lot with his

---

[408] Antony was then the sole boss of the senate.

[409] This sentence is taken with reservation, as it appears to be corrupt. The words preceding *provinciarum* are not clear. Ortman's edition of the text supplies *omissa cura provinciarum*, which I have followed. One manuscript has *destituta tutela provinciarum*, which carries the same basic meaning. But words preceding *provinciarum* do not appear in some manuscripts, and *provincia* can mean "province" as well as "office," "command," or "responsibility." The Chambers text seems to interpret *provinciarum* as "provinces" instead of duties of office.

[410] The modern city of Modena.

adversaries and hoped to gain some advantage by harming him. They also set out to rob his wife Fulvia of all her belongings, and were laying plans to kill Antony's children.

Although Atticus was on intimate terms with Cicero and remained a close personal friend of Brutus, he would not participate in any effort to strike out at Antony. On the contrary, he shielded Antony's friends as best he could as they fled Rome, and assisted them with whatever they needed. He provided such help to Publius Volumnius that more could not have come from a father. He showed such consideration in helping Fulvia when she was hounded by litigation and plagued by unremitting fear, that she was never present at a bail hearing in court without Atticus. He always acted as her bondsman. She had once bought a parcel of land during good times that had to be paid off by a certain due date; after disaster struck, she could not find a second lender to pay off the original obligation. Atticus then intervened, and lent her the money without interest or any formal statement of repayment terms: for him the greatest reward was to be known as considerate and appreciative. At the same time, he wanted to make it clear that for him what mattered was being a friend to others, not to their money.

By doing this, no one could say that he was acting as an obsequious opportunist, for no one then thought Antony would ever be able to return to power. Eventually he was condemned by a few nobles for not hating certain bad citizens with the required level of intensity. But Atticus was a man who made his own decisions, and his priority was to do what he believed was right, rather than what would be applauded by others.

10. Then a reversal of fortune unexpectedly came. Antony came back to Italy, and everyone thought that Atticus would be in great danger because of his closeness to Cicero and Brutus. Fearing proscription, he therefore left politics just as the generals arrived and quietly withdrew to Publius Volumnius's house. As I mentioned earlier, this was the man whom Atticus had earlier

helped. How great was the variability of fortune in those days, in that now some men, and now others, were either at the pinnacle of success or caught in the jaws of danger! With Atticus was Quintus Gellius Canus, a man much like himself and of comparable age. This is further proof of Atticus's essential goodness: he lived so closely with this man whom he had known in school as a boy, that their bonds of friendship grew even stronger as they reached old age.

Antony, however, so burned with hatred for Cicero that he saw not just him as an enemy, all of Cicero's friends as well, and very much wanted to proscribe them. There were many who encouraged Antony in these sentiments, but he did not forget the assistance that Atticus had previously given. So when he found out where Atticus was hiding, he wrote to him personally, saying he should not be afraid and asking him to come see him right away. He told Atticus he had removed his name, and Gellius Canus's[411] name, from the rolls of those who had been proscribed. Antony sent Atticus an armed escort so that no harm would come to him—as this sort of thing was known to happen at night.

Thus Atticus—who was in great fear—protected not only himself, but also the man who was closest to him. He did not ask for help from anyone for his own exclusive safety; he wanted it known that he sought no good fortune that was not shared by his friend.[412] But if special praise comes to that captain who saves his ship from a storm and rocky seas, should we not think that he who steers a course to safety through so many and such extreme civil upheavals is also possessed of remarkable prudence?

11. After he escaped all these terrible situations, Atticus had no desire to do anything except to help as many people as he could in whatever way he could manage it. Although the rabble hunted the proscribed with an eye to the rewards offered by the generals,

---

[411] Some manuscripts have "for his sake" (*illius causa*) before Gellius Canus.
[412] This sentence appears in the Chambers text, but not in Ortmann.

anyone who came to Epirus received all he needed; everyone was given the opportunity to stay there permanently. After the battle of Philippi and the deaths of Caius Cassius and Marcus Brutus, Atticus tried to protect the praetor Lucius Julius Mocilla and his son, along with Aulus Torquatus and the rest who were enduring the same hardships: anything these people needed, Atticus ordered, should be sent from Epirus to Samothrace.[413]

It is difficult to list all the specifics, and it is unnecessary to do so. This point I do wish to be understood: his generosity was not based on self-interest or manipulation. This fact can be clearly observed from the specific situations and from the times; he never licked the boots of the powerful, but always helped those who were suffering. He treated Brutus's mother Servilia with no less consideration after Brutus's death, than what he had extended during her time of good fortune. By consistently showing this sort of kindness to others, he made no real enemies. He harmed no one; and if he happened to be harmed by someone else, his response was to forget it rather than seek revenge.[414] He retained a permanent memory of generosity that had been extended to him by others; but with regard to a charitable act he himself performed, he remembered it only as long as the beneficiary was grateful. Thus he acted in accordance with the saying,

Each man's personal habits shape his own fortune.[415]

Nevertheless, before Atticus shaped his fortune, he shaped himself with enough protective traits to avoid ever being justly harmed.[416]

---

[413] Samothrace is an island in the northern Aegean Sea.

[414] This clause has a nice play on words in the original with the verbs "forget" and "seek revenge": *si quam iniuriam acceperat, non malebat oblivisci quam ulcisci.*

[415] The writer of this verse is not known.

[416] Meaning he incorporated cautionary traits in his character, so that he would be able to avoid putting himself in dangerous positions.

12. In this way Atticus caused Marcus Vipsanius Agrippa[417] (who was connected to the young Caesar[418] in a close friendship) to choose an affinity by marriage with Atticus's family over all others, and to prefer the daughter of a Roman knight over a woman from an aristocratic family. Even though he could have selected any bride he wished—due to his own interest and Caesar's power—Agrippa decided to make this choice. And the facilitator of this marriage—the fact should not be omitted—was Marcus Antonius, the triumvir for restructuring the republic. Although Antony's power could have augmented his wealth, Atticus's motives were so far from being based on money that he never used his connection with Antony except when trying to save his friends from danger or trouble.

This truth was abundantly clear during the time of the proscriptions. Lucius Saufeius—a Roman knight who was the same age as Atticus—had lived in Athens for several years to pursue philosophical studies, and owned expensive property in Italy. The triumvirs auctioned off his estate in the typical way things were done in those days. And because of Atticus's effort and diligence, Saufeius heard about both the loss, and the recovery, of his patrimony from the same messenger. Atticus also interceded on behalf of Lucius Julius Calidus,[419] who I truly believe may be the most elegant poet our age has produced since the deaths of Lucretius and Catullus, as well as being a man of good character and learned in the most refined arts. After the proscriptions of the knights, Calidus (then absent from Italy) was added to the proscription list by Publius Volumnius, Antony's praefect of engineers, because of Calidus's large property holdings in Africa. But Atticus intervened to save him. It is difficult to determine whether Atticus's

---

[417] He lived from 63 B.C. to 12 B.C.
[418] This is, of course, Caius Octavianus (Octavian), who later became the first emperor, Caesar Augustus.
[419] Nothing of his work survives.

actions were more laborious at the time, or more glorious,[420] since it was understood that his friends in their dangers were just as much in his care when they were absent, as when they were present.

13. Neither was this good man reckoned any less honorable as a father of a family than he was as a citizen. Although he was affluent, there was no one who was less enamored with the act of buying or building. Nevertheless, he lived in a very comfortable residence, and enjoyed the best of everything. He owned the house built by Tamphilus on the Quirinal Hill, a property he inherited from his uncle; the home's attractiveness derived not from the structure itself, but from the surrounding grove of trees. The house itself was very old, and in overall tone was more subdued than lavish. He made no attempt to change the house, unless its advanced age forced him to do so.

He had domestic servants who were extremely good, if we may judge by their usefulness, yet hardly average if we may judge by their personal appearance. Among them were some very learned slaves, some expert readers,[421] and a large number of copyists; in Atticus's household there was not even a lowly manservant[422] who could not admirably perform these literary duties. In the same way, the other craftsmen required for the maintenance of a household were of the greatest competence. All of Atticus's slaves were born in his home and trained there; this fact is an indication not only of his restraint, but also of his diligence. Not unreasonably craving what you see many others craving ought to be seen as evidence of strong personal discipline; and to obtain things through diligence rather than payment is no small indication of assiduity. He was elegant, not extravagant; impressive, not sumptuous; and he sought, with all his diligence,

---

[420] Meaning, it is not clear whether Atticus's actions caused him more trouble than the glory (renown) he received from them.
[421] The word used is *anagostes*, a slave trained to read aloud.
[422] *Pedisequus*, a male attendant or footman.

orderliness rather than affluent disarray.[423] His home furnishings were restrained, not excessive, so that they stood out neither way.

Although I expect there will be some who consider it unimportant, I will not fail to mention this: despite being one of the wealthiest Roman knights, and with considerable generosity inviting men of all social classes to his house, we know from reviewing Atticus's household budget record[424] that he regularly did not spend more than three thousand sesterces[425] per month. I say this from first-hand knowledge, not as something I heard from someone else: because of our close friendship, I often had direct involvement with his household affairs.

14. No one at one of his dinner parties ever heard any form of entertainment except a reader, which I believe is the most congenial; and never was there a formal meal in his house without some type of reading, so that his guests' minds, as well as their stomachs, left feeling satisfied. For he invited those whose inclinations were not inconsistent with his own. When that considerable enlargement was made to his financial holdings,[426] he changed nothing in his daily routine, and nothing in his basic lifestyle. In fact, he exercised such self-control that he lived a quite comfortable life on the two million sesterces he had inherited from his father; and he did not live more lavishly on ten million sesterces than he had lived before. He kept his lifestyle at the same level with both fortunes.

---

[423] A beautiful sentence. *Elegans, non magnificus, splendidus, non sumptuosus; omnisque diligentia munditiam, non adfluentiam adfectabat.*

[424] *Ephemeris*, a financial journal or diary. It was not uncommon for Romans to keep household budget records.

[425] Ortmann has *terna milia aeris* (i.e., three thousand asses) as the amount of money. Chambers omits the word *aeris*, with the assumption that "sesterces" is the better reading. We must agree with him. Three thousand asses would have been a very small sum of money, hardly sufficient for any kind of monthly entertainment expense.

[426] The inheritance received from his uncle, mentioned above.

He did not have any gardens,[427] or a sumptuous villa in the suburbs or by the ocean. He had no estate in the Italian countryside except his land in Arretium and Nomentum.[428] His financial revenue was dependent on his holdings in Epirus and Rome itself. One can easily understand from this that Atticus was accustomed to allocating his finances according to rational principles; he did not carelessly rely on the volume of wealth he possessed.

15. He never uttered lies, nor could he tolerate their utterance. Thus his courtesy was not without some strictness, and his seriousness not without some levity, so that it was not easy for his friends to know whether he should be feared or loved. When a favor was requested of him, he was cautious about committing himself, because he believed that to promise what one could not deliver was not generosity, but caprice. And in implementing what he had agreed to do, he was so diligent that he seemed to be taking care of his own interest, rather than someone else's. He never lost interest in performing a task he agreed to carry out; for he believed his own credibility was invested in his promises, and he valued nothing more than this.

It was on account of this impeccable reputation that he managed all the business dealings of the Ciceros, Marcus Cato, Quintus Hortensius, Aulus Torquatus, and many other Roman knights. One may conclude from this that Atticus shied away from government service not from laziness, but in order to avoid conflicts of interest.[429]

---

[427] As did the historian Sallust, for example.

[428] Arretium is now Arezzo in eastern Etruria; Nomentum is now Mentana.

[429] *Ex quo iudicari poterat non inertia, sed iudicio fugisse rei publicae procurationem.* Another reading of this sentence could be, "One may conclude from this that Atticus avoided government posts not from laziness, but out of good judgment." But I have chosen to translate *iudicio* in a way that emphasizes conflicts of interest, because the sentence's meaning aims at this issue. Becoming too involved in government service could set Atticus up for conflict of interest problems. He wisely did not want to be acting as a trustee or fiduciary for people whom he might have to oppose politically at some point.

16. I can present no better evidence of his good nature than to point out that as a youth he was much appreciated by Sulla, who was then advanced in years. When Atticus had himself aged, the young Marcus Brutus was very close to him. And with those of roughly his same age—Quintus Hortensius and Marcus Cicero—his dealings with them were such that it was difficult to tell what phase of life best suited him. Cicero so particularly valued Atticus that not even the orator's brother Quintus was to him dearer or more trusted. Verification of this is provided by the sixteen volumes of letters sent to Atticus covering the period from Cicero's consulate up to the end of his life.

Whoever reads these letters will not much wish for a formal history of those times.[430] Everything of importance is presented about the intentions of the era's major players, the flaws of the commanders, and the government's power shifts, to the extent that nothing is left ambiguous. One could easily arrive at the conclusion that Cicero's power of judgment was almost prophetic. For not only did he anticipate what would happen in his lifetime: he predicted, with the canniness of a fortune-teller, the events that are unfolding right now.

17. What more should I add about Atticus's sense of loyalty to others? I heard him say with pride at his mother's funeral—who was buried in her ninetieth year when he himself was sixty-seven—that he never had a reason to make peace with his mother, and never had a cause for enmity with his sister, who was approximately his same age. This anecdote shows that either there never was any quarrel between them, or that he was so patient with them that he considered it an impious act to hold grudges against those whom he ought to love. Nor did he behave this way because of Nature only, even though we all follow her commands: his conduct was the result of disciplined practice. He so thoroughly grasped the tenets of the major philosophers that he could apply

---

[430] These letters have survived, and this is an accurate statement.

this learning to real life, rather than just show off his knowledge for attention.[431]

18. He was a devoted follower of the old Roman customs, as well as a lover of antiquity in general. His learning in this regard was so comprehensive that he published a work describing the Roman magistrates in chronological sequence. No law, no peace treaty, no war, and no notable event of the Roman people has not been recorded at its correct date in this exhaustive work; and, what must have been most challenging, he has traced family lineages so meticulously that from his book we can determine the progenitors of our notable men. He dealt with this topic separately in other books.

At Marcus Brutus's request he enumerated the members of the Junii in correct order from the family's inception down to the present day, describing the lineage of each member, the public offices he held, and the dates in which he held them. He did the same thing for Claudius Marcellus with regard to the Marcelli family, for Cornelius Scipio with the Aemilii, and for Fabius Maximus with the Fabii. For those interested in learning about the lives of illustrious men, there can be nothing more pleasurable than poring over these volumes.

He also tried his hand at poetry, and I believe his motivation was to acquaint himself with its allure. He memorialized in verse those who outshone the rest of the Roman people in excellence and singularity of achievement; below the bust[432] of each man, he described their important deeds and offices in not more than four

---

[431] A fine sentence using a bit of word-play: *Nam principum philosophorum ita percepta habuit praecepta, ut iis ad vitam agendam, non ad ostentationem uteretur.*

[432] Atticus apparently had portraits or busts (the word used is *imagines*) of famous men in his residence, to which he affixed verses summarizing their deeds.

or five verses. That he was able to relate such information so compactly could scarcely be believed. He also composed a work in Greek on the consulship of Cicero.

19. The preceding sections constitute the portrait of Atticus I composed during his lifetime. Now since Fortune has resolved that I should outlive him, I wish to conclude my outline of his life; and through the use of specific examples, I will demonstrate as best I can that, for the most part, *every man's character traits*[433] *determine the trajectory of his life*. Atticus was satisfied with the social rank into which he was born, which was that of a Roman knight. He secured a relationship by marriage with the emperor (the deified Julius's son), although before this he had earned his friendship with nothing else except the studied gentility of his life, with which he had also captivated the other great men of Rome who were of comparable character but humbler fortune. For Caesar enjoyed such abundance that Fortune granted him everything that had been bestowed on his predecessors, and obtained for him what no other Roman citizen has thus far been able to acquire.

Atticus also had a grand-daughter fathered by Agrippa, whom he had arranged for his maiden daughter to marry. When the infant girl was hardly a year old, Caesar consented for her to be married to his stepson Tiberius Claudius Nero, the son of Drusilla. This contract ratified their bond of friendship, and increased the regularity of their association.

20. Not only when he was absent from the city, Octavian (even before this marriage contract was arranged) never wrote to anyone without first sending a letter to Atticus to let him know what he was doing, especially what he was reading, where he was, and how long he would be there. And when Octavian was in Rome (and although because of his many responsibilities he could not enjoy Atticus's company as much as he wanted), hardly a day

---

[433] Nepos uses the word *mores*, which can mean habits, character, behavior, or morals. "Character traits" best suits the context. This is an important sentence, for it reflects the attitude of many classical writers on the fateful connection between character and destiny.

passed in which Octavian did not write to him, asking some question related to antiquity, or offering up some poetical passage for literary interpretation. Sometimes joking with Atticus would elicit longer letters.

Their relationship was so close that when the temple of Jupiter Feretrius—built on the Capitol by Romulus—became exposed[434] and went to ruin as a consequence of age and neglect, Caesar, acting on Atticus's advice, saw to it that the temple was promptly repaired. Atticus was no less cultivated in literary correspondence by Mark Antony, when he was away from Rome. Indeed, from the ends of the earth Antony kept Atticus regularly informed of his activities and what his cares were. What this was like[435] will be better grasped by someone who can imagine how much acumen is needed to maintain the trust and favor of two men, between whom existed not only a rivalry for the most momentous things, but also a reciprocal effort to malign each other.[436] It was unavoidable that this would happen between Caesar and Antony, since each of them wanted to be the ruler not only of Rome, but of the entire world.

21. He finished seventy-seven years in this way, and until very old age he grew no less in dignity than he did in esteem and good fortune. Indeed, he collected many inheritances for no other reason than his moral excellence; and he enjoyed such soundness of health that he needed no attention from a physician for thirty years. But then Atticus developed a condition which both he and his doctor did not take seriously; they thought it was tenesmus,[437]

---

[434] By losing its roof.
[435] I.e., how much effort it took to stay on good terms with both Antony and Octavian.
[436] There is nice word play here between *aemulatio* (rivalry) and *obtrectatio* (disparagement, detraction).
[437] The word used is *tenesmos* (or *tenesmus*), which the Oxford Latin Dictionary defines as a "griping pain in the bowels, accompanied by ineffectual

a problem for which cursory and straightforward treatments could be obtained. After enduring this condition for three months without any pain except for what he had experienced from the doctor's regimen, the disease suddenly erupted from the depth of his intestines with such intensity that fistulas leaking corrupt matter emerged from his loins.

Before these events took place, after feeling his pain and fever getting worse day by day, he ordered his son-in-law Agrippa to be brought to him, along with Lucius Cornelius Balbus[438] and Sextus Peducaeus.[439] When he saw they were before him, Atticus propped himself up on his forearm and said, "Since you've seen what has been happening,[440] it is hardly necessary for me to speak at length about the degree of care and effort I have given to preserving my health at this time. With these efforts, I hope I've satisfied you that there is nothing left for me to do that might halt my decline. The only remaining thing is for me to take the appropriate measures for my situation. I didn't want you to be left in the dark: I have decided to stop feeding the disease. Whatever food I've eaten in recent days has prolonged my life in a way that only adds to my suffering, without providing any hope of recovery. So

---

straining." Rolfe's 1929 translation renders this term as "dysentery," a reading which may be questioned. Pliny (*Hist. Nat.* XX.86) draws a distinction between sufferers of dysentery (*dysinterici*) and its opposite, *tenesmus*. He writes, "Hippocrates advised cabbage cooked twice with salt as a remedy for sufferers of bowel disorders and dysentery, and the same for tenesmus and kidney problems…" (*Hippocrates coeliacis et dysintericis bis coctam cum sale, item ad tenesmum et renium causa*). Pliny makes it clear that tenesmus is the inability to excrete waste, which is essentially the opposite of dysentery. He defines tenesmus as "the frequent and futile desire to excrete waste" (*tenesmus, id est crebra et inanis voluntas desurgendi*). See Nat. Hist. XXVIII.211.

[438] Consul in 40 B.C.

[439] Propraetor in Spain in 39 B.C.

[440] *Cum vos testes habeam,* literally, "Since I have you as witnesses."

I ask you first to accept my decision; finally, that you not waste your time trying to talk me out of it."

22. Once he had uttered these words with such resolution of voice and countenance that he appeared not to be departing this life, but rather migrating from one abode to another, Agrippa, now pressing kisses on Atticus with tear-flushed eyes, begged and pleaded with him not to accelerate on his own that which nature had set in motion, and, since he still might be able to overcome his condition, to stay alive for his own sake and for the sake of his family. Yet Atticus dismissed these pleadings with an unyielding muteness.

After he had gone without food for two days, his fever suddenly went away and the disease began to subside. Yet Atticus still wished to follow through with his intention. The end came on the fifth day after he had decided to refuse food. This was the day before the Calends of April, during the consulship of Cnaeus Domitius and Caius Sosius.[441] He was brought out for burial in a small litter, as he had instructed, without any ostentatious funeral ceremony. All the good citizens, and a large crowd of the general public, were there to pay their respects. He was laid to rest in the tomb of his maternal uncle Quintus Caecilius, near the fifth milestone along the Appian Way.

---

[441] March 31, 32 B.C. The first day of the month was called Kalendae (Calends).

Fragments, Testimonies, and Judgments

Translator's Note: Below is a selection of quotations referring to Nepos written by various classical authors. Following this are surviving fragments of Nepos's writing.

TESTIMONIES AND JUDGMENTS

Regarding Homer and Hesiod, nearly all writers agree that…both lived before the founding of Rome…but as Cornelius Nepos says about Homer in the first book of his *Chronicles*, about a hundred and sixty years before the founding of Rome. [Aulus Gellius, *Attic Nights* XVII.21.3]

However, Cornelius Nepos says that Archilochus was already well-known and distinguished for his poetry when Tullus Hostilius was king at Rome. [Aulus Gellius XVII.21.8]

"Tell me, I ask you," he said, "who forced you to do what you want to seek a pardon for, even before you have done it?" This is stated in the thirteenth book of Cornelius Nepos's *On Illustrious Men*. [Aulus Gellius XI.8.5]

Many have wrongly stated this, including Nepos, who lived along the course of the Po; for no river flows out of the Danube into the Adriatic Sea. [Pliny, *Hist. Nat.* III.127]

Cornelius Nepos was scrupulous in the use of written sources, and was one of Marcus Cicero's closest friends. Nevertheless, in the first book of the biography he composed on Cicero's life, he apparently made a mistake in writing that Cicero presented his first case at trial when he was twenty-three years of age, when he defended Sextus Roscius, who was charged with parricide. [Aulus Gellius XV.28]

This is what some of the old writers were afraid of…just as Cicero, a reliable witness, affirms in a letter to Cornelius Nepos. [Ammianus Marcellinus, *Res Gestae* XXVI.1.2]

Then becoming a professor of rhetoric, he [Manius Otacilius Pitholaus] gave instruction to Cnaeus Pompeius, and composed in several books an account of the deeds of Pompey's father, and also those of his son. Cornelius Nepos claims that he was the first emancipated slave to write history; before him the genre had been the exclusive province of men of the upper classes. [Suetonius, *On Rhetoricians* III]

In addition, Cornelius Nepos, in a small book that distinguishes *litteratus* and *eruditus*, claims that *litteratus* is colloquially intended to refer to those who can speak or write on any topic precisely, wittily, and knowledgeably. [Suetonius, *On Grammarians* IV]

In addition to the scientists and the poet Homer, who said that the known world was bounded by seas, Cornelius Nepos is a more reliable authority because he is of more recent date. [Pomponius Mela III.45]

Titus Livius and Cornelius Nepos claim that the width at the narrowest point is seven miles, and at the widest point is ten miles…[Pliny, *Nat. Hist.* III.4]

Cincius believes Rome was founded around the twelfth Olympiad; Pictor says the eighth; [Cornelius] Nepos and Lutatius adopt the view of Eratosthenes and Apollodorus, and date the founding to the second year of the seventh Olympiad. [Solinus, *Polyhistor* I]

FRAGMENTS

1. *Excerpt from a letter of Cornelia, the mother of the Gracchus brothers, from Cornelius Nepos's book on the Latin historians*:

You will say it is sweet to avenge oneself against one's enemies. That seems greater and sweeter to no one more than myself, but it is something that should only be done to safeguard the republic. But to the extent this is not possible, for a long time and without doubt our enemies will not die, but will persist as they are now, rather than that the republic will collapse and perish.

From the same letter:

I venture to affirm, in no uncertain terms, that except for those who killed Tiberius Gracchus, no enemy has given me as much stress and trouble on account of these things except you. As the only survivor of the children I have had, you should have stepped into their shoes and made sure that I had the least amount of worry in my old age. You should have wanted all your actions to be acceptable to me; and you should have thought it deeply wrong to do anything against my wishes, especially since my remaining years are so few in number. Can this short amount of time help me prevent you from fighting me and bringing down the republic? When will all this finally end? Will our family ever stop this insanity? When will there be a limit? When will we stop trying to cause or endure trouble? When will we be ashamed of implicating and tormenting our country?

But if this is completely hopeless, seek the tribunate when I have passed away. It is enough for me that you do as you please, since I will no longer know. When I have died, you will observe the rituals in honor of the dead, and will invoke our family gods.[442] Won't you be ashamed at that time to seek prayers from those as gods whom you tossed aside and discarded when they were still living? I hope Jupiter stops you from going down this road, and does not permit this insanity to enter your mind. And if you keep doing what you are doing, I fear that through your own fault, you will experience such problems for the rest of your life that you will never be able to alleviate your own guilt.

2. *Eulogy of Cicero, from Cornelius Nepos's book on the Latin historians.*

You should know this is the one type[443] of Latin literature that even now is unequal to its counterpart in Greek literature; with the death of Cicero it was left entirely rudimentary and unpolished. He was the only man who could compose—or even tried to compose—history with a worthy voice. He burnished the coarse expressiveness inherited from our ancestors; he imprinted Latin philosophy—which before him was graceless—with his own distinctive stamp. This makes me wonder whether his death inflicted more suffering on our country or on posterity.

3. *From the same text*:

To gain greater affection and better circulate her benevolence, fecund and divine Nature desires neither to give everything to one person, nor conversely to deny everything to any person.

---

[442] *Ubi mortua ero, parentabis mihi et invocabis deum parentem.* The verb *parentare* is to celebrate the *parentalia*, the festival in honor of the dead.
[443] The writing of history.

4. *Cornelius Nepos's letter to Cicero*:

I am so far from believing that philosophy can instruct us how to live, and acts as the agent of a happy life, that I think no one needs to learn how to live more than most of these people involved in teaching it. From what I see, a large part of those people in the schools who advocate most cleverly in favor of self-control and abstinence are the same ones living in thrall of all the appetites.[444]

---

[444] Found in Lactantius, *Inst. Div.* III.15.

INDEX

A

Acarnania, 48
Acheron, 122
Acropolis, 50, 51, 64, 77
Adimantus, 94
Admetus, 56, 57
Aegates Islands, 207
Aegean, 37, 63, 76, 129, 245
Aegiae, 204
Aegina, 49
Aegospotami, 80
Aegospotamoi, 97, 107
Aemilius Probus, 19, 198
Aeolia, 112
Aeolis, 37
Africa, 83, 195, 205, 208, 209, 210, 215, 220, 221, 229, 246
Agamemnon's, 153
Agesilaus, 22, 108, 110, 127, 128, 131, 166, 167, 168, 169, 171, 172, 173, 174, 175, 202
Agis, 166
Agrippa, 246, 252, 254, 255
Alcibiades, 26, 86, 87, 88, 89, 90, 91, 92, 93, 94, 97, 98, 99, 100, 102
Alcmaeon, 154
Alexander, 12, 125, 164, 165, 177, 178, 180, 181, 182, 187, 188, 204, 205
Alps, 215
Ammianus Marcellinus, 25, 257
Amyntas, 125, 176, 204
Andocides, 87
Antigenes, 180, 182
Antigonus, 180, 181, 182, 183, 184, 185, 186, 187, 188, 205
Antiochus, 94, 212, 213, 221, 222
Antipater, 177, 178, 179, 180, 189, 190
Antony, 169, 242, 243, 244, 246, 253
Apollo, 13, 35, 37, 50, 63, 67

Apollocrates, 118
Apollodorus, 258
Appian Way, 255
Apulia, 114, 216, 217
Aquilo, 36
Archias, 163
Archilochus, 256
Archinus, 163
Arete, 113, 116, 120
Argilus, 71
Argos, 56, 154, 204
Ariobarzanes, 131, 137, 141, 145
Aristides, 26, 62, 63, 65
Aristippus, 11
Aristomache, 113, 120
Armenians, 143
Arretium, 249
Arsinoe, 33
Artabanus, 203
Artabazus, 67, 71
Artaphernes, 40
Artaxerxes, 57, 58, 99, 108, 124, 128, 136, 138, 140, 142, 144, 151, 164, 167, 203
Artaxerxes Macrochir, 203
Artaxerxes Mnemon, 151, 164, 203
Artemisium, 50
Asdrubal, 195
Asia Minor, 24, 37, 38, 94, 98, 106, 108, 110, 131
Aspendus, 143
Aspis, 138, 140
Athamanes, 132
Athens, 21, 32, 33, 35, 36, 40, 41, 42, 43, 45, 49, 50, 51, 52, 53, 54, 56, 63, 64, 75, 77, 80, 87, 89, 92, 93, 97, 98, 99, 100, 103, 110, 115, 125, 127, 128, 132, 133, 134, 152, 162, 163, 189, 190, 191, 192, 234, 235, 236, 246
Attica, 40, 47, 56, 59, 92, 103, 105, 132, 154, 192

Atticus, 16, 18, 19, 20, 32, 225, 227, 232, 233, 234, 235, 236, 237, 240, 241, 242, 243, 244, 245, 246, 247, 248, 249, 250, 251, 252, 253, 254, 255
Aulus Gellius, 25, 77, 256, 257
Aulus Torquatus, 245, 249
Automatia, 198
Autophrodates, 136, 142, 143, 144

B

Barbarus, Franciscus, 13
Battle of Leuctra, 155
Battle of Nemea, 172
Bithynia, 222, 224
Bizanthe, 97
Boeotia, 41, 63, 83
Bolgius, 205
Bracciolini, Poggio, 13
Brutus, 241, 242, 243, 245
Byzantium, 67, 93

C

Cadmea, 159, 161, 163
Caesar, 12, 17, 169, 240, 241, 246, 252, 253
Caius Aurelius, 220
Caius Centenius, 216
Caius Claudius Nero, 228
Caius Flaminius, 216
Caius Flavius, 241
Caius Helvius, 228
Caius Lutatius, 207
Caius Marius, 233
Caius Sosius, 255
Caius Terentius, 216
Callias, 75
Callicrates, 120, 121
Calliphron, 149
Callistratus, 154
Camisares, 136
Campania, 216
Cannae, 24, 216, 217

Cappadocia, 136, 138, 141, 143, 177, 188
Captiani, 143
Capua, 216
Cardaces, 143
Cardia, 176
Caria, 58, 110, 168
Carians, 37
Carthage, 23, 114, 207, 208, 209, 213, 215, 217, 220, 221
Carthaginians, 19, 114, 134, 193, 195, 207, 208, 209, 220, 221
Cassander, 188, 190, 191
Cassius, 241, 242, 245
Catalonia, 232
Cataonia, 138
Cato, 17, 18, 19, 20, 227, 228, 229, 230, 231, 232, 249
Catullus, 17, 20, 246
Catulus, 207, 208
Ceprano, 220
Chabrias, 22, 127, 128, 129, 134, 152
Chaones, 132
Chares, 129, 132, 133, 190
Charon, 163
Chersonese, 176
Chersonesus, 35, 36, 40, 45
chiliarch, 108, 109
Chios, 100, 129
Chronica, 17
Cicero, Marcus Tullius, 17, 20, 23, 121, 243, 257, 259
Cilicia, 106, 136, 138, 140, 143
Cimon, 32, 33, 35, 75, 76, 77
Cinna, 234
Citium, 77
Clastidium, 215
clava, 68
Cleon, 83
Clinias, 86
Clytaemnestra, 154
Cnaeus Domitius, 255
Cnaeus Pompeius, 257
Cnidus, 110, 112
Codrus, 35

264

Colonae, 68
Conon, 21, 107, 108, 109, 110, 111, 112, 128, 131, 133
Corcyra, 49, 56, 132
Corinth, 115, 118, 124, 171, 172, 194, 195
Corinthian War, 171
Coronea, 86, 171
Cotus, 125, 131
Craterus, 177, 178, 179
Crete, 32, 222
Crinissus, 195
Crithote, 131
Critias, 99, 105
Cyclades, 37, 43, 57, 63
Cyme, 94
Cyprus, 67, 77, 127, 128
Cyrene, 175, 221
Cyrus, 99, 108, 202
Cyzicus, 131, 151

D

Damala, 50
Damon, 148
Danube, 37, 256
Dardanelles, 35
Darius, 37, 40, 49, 66, 92, 202
Datames, 21, 136, 137, 138, 139, 140, 141, 142, 143, 144, 145, 146, 202
Datis, 40, 42
Decelea, 92
Delos, 37, 63
Delphi, 35, 49, 66, 83
Demades's, 189
Demaenetus, 199
Demeter, 90
Demetrius of Phalerum, 43, 190
Demosthenes, 189, 190
Dercylus, 190
Diadochi, 178
Dinon, 19, 112
Diogenes Laertius, 11
Diomedon, 151, 152
Dion, 21, 23, 26, 113, 114, 115, 117, 118, 119, 120, 121, 122, 194

Dionysius, 19, 113, 114, 115, 118, 148, 194, 204
Dionysius Lambinus, 19
Dolopians, 76
Drusilla, 252

E

Egypt, 124, 127, 138, 140, 174, 175, 178, 205
Egyptians, 128
Elis, 90
Elpinice, 33, 75
Epaminondas, 20, 22, 26, 32, 124, 148, 149, 150, 151, 152, 153, 154, 155, 156, 157, 158, 159, 160, 164, 172
ephors, 53, 54, 68, 71, 84, 169
Epirotes, 132
Epirus, 56, 122, 181, 204, 242, 245, 249
Eratosthenes, 258
Eryx, 207, 208
Etruria, 216, 249
Euboea, 40, 50, 67, 133
Eumenes, 20, 23, 176, 177, 178, 179, 180, 181, 182, 183, 184, 185, 186, 187, 188, 202, 222, 223, 224
Eumolpidae, 90, 94
Euphiletus, 192
Eurybiades, 51
Eurydice, 125
Eurysthenes, 166, 173
Evagoras, 128
Exempla, 17

F

Falernum, 216
First Punic War, 207
fortune, 20, 21, 37, 38, 87, 93, 95, 102, 112, 119, 121, 128, 140, 164, 176, 181, 189, 193, 198, 204, 210, 226, 235, 243, 244, 245, 250, 252, 253
Fregellae, 220
Fulvia, 243

G

Galen, 12
gerusia, 54
Gnaeus Baebius Tamphilus, 225
Gnaeus Manlius Volso, 226
Gnaeus Servilius Geminus, 216
Gongylus, 67
Gortyna, 222
Gortynians, 222
Grynium, 98

H

Hadrumentum, 217, 218
Haliartus, 83
Hamilcar Barca, 26, 134, 195, 211
Hannibal, 19, 24, 26, 124, 134, 141, 205, 207, 209, 210, 212, 213, 215, 216, 217, 219, 220, 221, 222, 223, 224, 225, 226, 228
Hasdrubal, 209, 215, 228
Hellespont, 52, 57, 58, 67, 80, 93, 132, 171, 178, 180
helots, 69
Hephaestia, 36
Heraclides, 118, 119
Hercules, 166, 215
Hermes, 87
Herodotus, 37, 202
Hesiod, 256
Hicetas, 194
Hipparinus, 113
Hippo, 209
Hipponicus, 86
Hister, 37
Homer, 137, 256, 257
Hortensius, 237, 249, 250
Hydarnes, 203
Hystaspes, 202

I

Ibn Zafar al-Siqilli, 121
Ionia, 37, 58, 93, 107, 112, 129, 137

Iphicrates, 123, 124, 125, 128, 132, 133, 134
Ismenias, 164

J

Jason, 134
Jupiter, 83, 213, 253, 259

K

Kassandra, 161

L

Lacedaemon, 53, 72, 83, 90
Lacedaemonians, 32, 41, 50, 52, 53, 54, 56, 63, 67, 68, 69, 71, 77, 80, 83, 92, 93, 97, 98, 99, 101, 103, 107, 109, 110, 124, 128, 132, 154, 155, 157, 158, 159, 161, 162, 167, 169, 172, 173
Laconia, 71
Lactantius, 260
Lamachus, 87
Lamprus, 148
Lampsacus, 58
Laphystius, 198
Lapseki, 58
later, 42, 63, 72, 93, 100, 105, 127, 134, 138, 155, 190, 217, 246
Lemnos, 36, 37
Leonidas, 50
Leonnatus, 178
Leotychides, 166
Leucosyri, 136
Leuctra, 154, 157, 158, 162, 164, 172, 173
Liguria, 216
Lucius Aemilius, 216, 225
Lucius Cornelius, 221, 254
Lucius Cotta, 236
Lucius Furius, 221
Lucius Julius Calidus, 246
Lucius Saufeius, 246
Lucius Torquatus, 233, 236

Lucius Valerius Flaccus, 228, 229
Lusitanians, 232
Lycia, 106
Lyco, 122
Lycus, 93, 102
Lysander, 26, 80, 81, 82, 83, 84, 85, 94, 97, 98, 99, 107, 110, 167
Lysimachus, 62, 185, 205

M

Macedonia, 76, 125, 161, 178, 179, 181, 191
Maeander, 58
Magna Graecia, 90, 114
Magnesia, 58, 141
Mago, 220, 221
Mamercus, 195
Mandrocles, 141
Mantinea, 158
mantlet, 43
Marathon, 40, 42, 49, 52, 53
Marcus Acilius Glabrio, 221
Marcus Baebius Tamphilus, 225
Marcus Brutus, 241, 245, 250, 251
Marcus Claudius, 217, 220, 225, 228
Marcus Claudius Marcellus, 217, 225
Marcus Minucius Rufus, 217
Marcus Perpenna, 228
Marcus Vipsanius Agrippa, 246
Mardonius, 63, 66
Marmara, 98
Matapan, 71
Media, 136, 182, 183
Megaris, 192
Meneclides, 153
Menelaus, 175
Menestheus, 132
Messagetae, 202, 203
Messene, 157, 164
Messenia, 107
Micythus, 152
Miltiades, 19, 21, 35, 36, 37, 40, 41, 42, 43, 45, 46, 56, 75
Minerva, 72, 171
Mithridates, 140, 145, 146

Mithrobarzanes, 141, 142
Mnestheus, 125
Molossians, 56
Münster, Sebastian, 26, 39, 60, 73, 126, 130, 200, 206, 214
Munychia, 105
Mutina, 242
Mycale, 76
Myrian, 36
Mytilene, 106
Myus, 58

N

Nectenebis, 127, 175
Neocles, 48
Neontichos, 97
Nicanor, 190, 191
Nicias, 87
Nisaeus, 113
Nomentum, 249

O

Octavian, 169, 246, 252, 253
Olympia, 33, 94
Olympias, 181
Olympiodorus, 149
Olynthians, 131
Olynthus, 161
Onomarchus, 186
Orchomenians, 83
Orestes, 154
Origines, 231
Orni, 97
Ortygia, 118
Ostiglia, 16

P

Pactye, 97
palaestra, 149
Palestine, 174
Pamphylia, 106, 143
Pamphylian Sea, 222
Pandantes, 140

parmae, 123
Paros, 43, 45
Parysatis, 203
Patroclus, 137
Pausanias, 26, 63, 66, 67, 68, 69, 71, 72, 74, 105, 125, 204
Pavia, 16
Pelopidas, 21, 155, 158, 161, 162, 163, 164, 165
Peloponnesian War, 80, 86, 87, 102, 103, 107, 162
Peloponnesus, 53, 107, 115, 120, 122, 132, 155, 157, 158, 171, 204
peltae, 123
penates, 54
Perdiccas, 125, 177, 178, 180
Pericles, 86
Persephone, 90
Persia, 23, 56, 58, 92, 164, 169, 182
Persians, 42, 43, 49, 50, 66, 67, 101, 128, 143, 172, 174, 175
Perugia, 216
Peucestes, 181
phalanx, 164, 182
Phalerum, 52, 191
Pharnabazus, 83, 84, 98, 99, 100, 107, 108, 109, 110, 138
Pherae, 107, 164
Phidippus, 41
Philip, 125, 132, 176, 177, 181, 187, 189, 191, 204, 212
Philippi, 245
Philippus, 125
Philistus, 115
Philo of Alexandria, 32
Philocles, 97
Philostratus, 121
Phocion, 189, 190, 192
Phoebidas, 161
Phoenicia, 174
Phrygia, 98, 99, 107, 131, 137, 144, 168, 180
Phyle, 103, 105
Pictor, 258
Piraeus, 52, 93, 105, 110, 190, 191

Pisander, 92, 110
Pisistratus, 45
Pittacus, 106
Plataea, 63, 66, 67
Plataeans, 41
Plato, 87, 114, 115
Pliny, 16, 25, 254, 256, 257
Plutarch, 11, 17, 20, 25, 33, 62, 148, 203
Po, 16, 215, 217, 256
Poicile, 42
polemarchs, 163
Polybius, 19, 24, 225
Polymnis, 148
Polyperchon, 191
Pompey, 241, 257
Pomponius Mela, 257
Pontus, 222
potsherds, 56, 62
Praeda, 77
Procles, 166
Propontis, 98, 131
Prusias, 222, 224
Ptolemaeus Ceraunus, 205
Ptolemy, 33, 178, 185, 188, 205
Ptolemy I Soter, 205
Ptolemy III Euergetes, 205
Ptolemy IV Philopator, 205
Ptolemy Philadelphus, 33, 205
Publius Cornelius Cethegus, 225
Publius Cornelius Scipio, 215, 228
Publius Scipio Africanus, 229
Publius Sulpicius, 220, 234
Publius Volumnius, 243, 246
pulvinar, 132
Pydna, 57
Pylaemenes, 137
Pyrenees, 215
Pyrrhus, 204
Pythia, 35, 49

Q

Quintilian, 12
Quintus Caecilius, 236, 255
Quintus Cicero, 237, 240, 241

Quintus Fabius Maximus, 124, 216
Quintus Gellius Canus, 244
Quintus Minucius, 221
Quintus Tullius Cicero, 237

R

Red Sea, 212

S

Sacred Band, 164
Saguntum, 215
Salamis, 50, 51, 52, 53, 57, 63, 128
Sallust, 1, 25, 168, 249
Samos, 92, 93, 131, 132, 133
Sardis, 40, 112, 168
Saros, 176
Sart, 40
Scipio, 215, 217, 228, 229, 251
Seleucus, 180, 185, 188, 205
Servius Galba, 232
Sestus, 131
Seuthes, 97, 124
Seven Sages, 106
Sextus Peducaeus, 254
Sicily, 89, 92, 93, 114, 118, 120, 122, 193, 194, 195, 198, 199, 200, 207, 208, 228
Sigeum, 129
Silenus, 19, 226
Social War, 125, 129
Socrates, 86, 166
Sophrosyne, 113
Sosilus, 19
Sosylus, 226
Spain, 209, 210, 213, 215, 229, 232, 254
Sparta, 22, 33, 41, 53, 54, 67, 68, 71, 80, 92, 93, 108, 125, 154, 157, 164, 166, 169, 172, 175
Sporades, 76
Stateira, 203
Stesagoras, 45
Strymon, 76
Suetonius, 25, 257

suffes, 220
Sulla, 169, 234, 235, 236, 250
Sulpicius Blitho, 19, 225
Symposium, 87
Syracuse, 87, 113, 114, 115, 118, 119, 195, 196, 204
Syria, 212, 221

T

Tachos, 174
Taenarum, 71
Tagus, 209
Tamphilus, 247
Tarentum, 114, 149
Tarkumuwa, 139
Taurus, 108, 140, 178
tenesmus, 253
Thasians, 76, 81
Thasos, 76, 81
Thebes, 90, 100, 127, 151, 152, 157, 158, 159, 161, 162, 163, 164
Themistocles, 26, 48, 49, 50, 51, 52, 53, 55, 56, 57, 58, 62, 64
Theopompus, 19, 100, 125
Theramenes, 93
Thermopylae, 50, 51, 221
Thessaly, 134, 155, 164, 190
Thrace, 76, 97, 98, 128, 131, 205
Thrasybulus, 23, 93, 94, 102, 103, 104, 105, 106
Thucydides, 19, 24, 48, 49, 57, 58, 67, 100
Thurii, 90
Thuys, 136, 137, 138
Tiberius Sempronius Gracchus, 217
Timaeus, 19, 100
Timoleon, 26, 193, 194, 195, 196, 197, 198, 201
Timoleonteum, 199
Timophanes, 193, 194
Timotheus, 21, 125, 128, 131, 132, 133, 134
Tiribazus, 112
Tissaphernes, 92, 107, 108, 109, 167, 168

Titus Livius, 257
Titus Quinctius Flaminius, 224
Trasimene, 216
Trebia, 215, 217
Troad, 68
Troezene, 50
Trojan War, 137, 153
Tusculum, 228, 230

U

Utica, 209

V

Valencia, 232

Venusia, 217
Vergerio, Paolo, 12
Vettones, 210

X

Xenophon, 19, 166
Xerxes, 49, 51, 52, 57, 62, 66, 67, 171, 203

Z

Zacynthos, 121
Zama, 217, 218
Zeno, 42

www.ingramcontent.com/pod-product-compliance
Lightning Source LLC
Chambersburg PA
CBHW060641150426
42811CB00078B/2237/J